the
Ice Cream
bible

Marilyn Linton & Tanya Linton

Robert
ROSE

The Ice Cream Bible
Text copyright © 2008 Marilyn Linton and Tanya Linton
Cover and text design copyright © 2008 Robert Rose Inc.
Photographs copyright © 2008 Robert Rose Inc.

Some of the material in this book was previously published in *125 Best Ice Cream Recipes*,
published by Robert Rose Inc. in 2003.

For complete cataloguing information, see page 265.

Disclaimer
The recipes in this book have been carefully tested by our kitchen and our tasters. To the best of
our knowledge, they are safe and nutritious for ordinary use and users. For those people with food
or other allergies, or who have special food requirements or health issues, please read the suggested
contents of each recipe carefully and determine whether or not they may create a problem for you.
All recipes are used at the risk of the consumer.

We cannot be responsible for any hazards, loss or damage that may occur as a result of any
recipe use.

For those with special needs, allergies, requirements or health problems, in the event of
any doubt, please contact your medical advisor prior to the use of any recipe.

Design & Production: Daniella Zanchetta/PageWave Graphics Inc.
Editors: Carol Sherman and Sue Sumeraj
Recipe Tester: Jennifer MacKenzie
Proofreader: Sheila Wawanash
Indexer: Gillian Watts
Photography: Colin Erricson and Mark T. Shapiro
Food Stylists: Kate Bush and Kathryn Robertson
Props Stylist: Charlene Erricson

The publisher and authors wish to express their appreciation to the following supplier of props
used in some of the food photography:
DISHES, LINENS AND ACCESSORIES
Homefront
371 Eglinton Ave. West, Toronto, Ontario M5N 1A3
Tel: (416) 488-3189   www.homefrontshop.com

Cover image: Raspberry-Blackberry Ice Cream (page 66)

We acknowledge the financial support of the Government of Canada through the Book Publishing
Industry Development Program (BPIDP) for our publishing activities.

Published by Robert Rose Inc.
120 Eglinton Ave. E., Suite 800, Toronto, Ontario, Canada M4P 1E2
Tel: (416) 322-6552   Fax: (416) 322-6936

Printed in Canada
1 2 3 4 5 6 7 8 9 10   TCP   13 12 11 10 09 08 07

the
Ice Cream
bible

Contents

Acknowledgments

WRITING A COOKBOOK IS A LABOR OF LOVE. Ideas need to be brainstormed. Ingredients need to be researched, and, most importantly, recipes need to be tested and tasted. We discovered that with ice cream as a topic, it wasn't very hard to find eager tasters to lick, slurp and sample various scoops. We couldn't have gotten through any of the stages of this book without the help of so many people.

For starters, this book would never have come to a freezer section near you if it weren't for the support of Bob Dees and the Robert Rose creative team. Thank you to our editors, Carol Sherman and Sue Sumeraj, whose impressive patience (working with two Linton ladies), diligent editing and coordinating of the manuscript helped to take us from ice cream dreams to reality. Thanks also to Jennifer MacKenzie, whose knowledge of testing enabled us to fine-tune our recipes, and to proofreader Sheila Wawanash.

Of course, a cookbook just isn't the same without photos, and for those we are grateful to photographers Colin Erricson and Mark Shapiro, props stylist Charlene Erricson and food stylists Kate Bush and Kathryn Robertson, whose talents for preparing ice cream for use under hot lights cannot be underestimated. Thanks, too, to designer Daniella Zanchetta at PageWave Graphics.

We had help in researching the science of ice cream. The Department of Food Science at the University of Guelph in Ontario was of great assistance. We would also like to thank Cuisinart for giving us ice cream makers so that we could whip up many of the desserts in this book.

We were also very fortunate to have Jim Borwick, a family friend, whose creative input and recipe testing we relied on when we thought we had hit the ice cream wall. And last, but certainly not least, a big thank you goes out to our family, Doug Linton, Mike Sheerin, Sam Linton, Robert Meynell, Charley Borwick and Sasha Borwick, who never tired of sampling and resampling the flavors found in this book.

Introduction

LIKE EVERYONE ELSE IN THE WORLD, WE LOVE ICE CREAM. Not only is it the ultimate comfort food, one that's associated with fond memories of summer vacations and birthday parties, but it's also the ultimate treat, a little luxury that's affordable and easily available virtually anywhere in the world today. Thanks to the various ice cream makers that are now on the market, it's also the ideal food to make at home.

While each commercial manufacturer boasts dozens of flavors, we discovered to our delight that our made-at-home list was virtually limitless. The smaller batches produced in home ice cream makers get your creative juices flowing by inviting frequent experimentation. In trying everything from Apple Brown Betty Ice Cream (see recipe, page 74) to Beet Apple Slush (see recipe, page 225), we found — as we're sure you will — that inventing new flavor combinations is half the fun.

And because home ice cream makers incorporate less air into the mixture during the churning process than traditional big-batch commercial machines do, you're sure to get an ice cream that's creamier and fresher than store-bought. Ice cream was always meant to be eaten fresh, and there are even some ice cream aficionados who believe that storing it in the freezer compromises the flavor. We found that keeping it in the freezer for several days or even a week or two doesn't detract from the flavor too much, but nothing beats the taste of ice cream straight out of the machine or just a few hours old.

We think one of the reasons why ice cream makers are increasingly popular is that more and more of us are concerned about the components of our food. Homemade ice cream and its cousins — sherbets and ices — are about as wholesome as you can get. Not only do you start with the freshest eggs, milk, fruit and/or flavorings, but also, because you select them, you can make sure the ingredients are exactly what you want.

You can make it organic if that's important, low-fat if weight or cholesterol is an issue, or nut-free if allergies are a concern. Healthwise, ice cream, though it is about 14% fat, is a good source of both protein and calcium — the latter is essential for building and maintaining healthy bones in all of us, whatever our age. As well, most North American supermarkets now carry a good range of low-fat dairy (and non-dairy) products that decrease fat content without sacrificing taste. (Frozen yogurt, introduced in the 1970s and perceived by some as healthier than regular ice cream, is also a make-at-home option, particularly since the flavors available at the supermarket are still limited.) In each of our recipes, you are building your ice cream from the ground up, not relying on a commercial mix (even many ice cream shops that claim to make their own start with a mix).

We also found that ice cream is no longer confined to traditional flavors or enjoyed only in a sugar cone after dinner. In our ice cream travels, we learned that the sky's the limit as far as flavors go (the Roasted Garlic Ice Cream on page 134 is surprisingly good) and that ice cream isn't just a dessert (our healthy Tomato Basil Ice on page 228 makes that clear, as does one of our favorite breakfasts, waffles with Banana Ice Cream, on page 98.) Our serving suggestions will show you how to enhance your ice cream to fit into a party theme or mood.

That ice cream is such a simple food belies the fact that, sciencewise, it's a complex structure of ice crystals and fat globules. When conditions are right, they combine to make a frozen mixture with a good "mouth feel" to it — that is, a smooth, consistent texture rather than a coarse, grainy one. In our recipes, we provide the proper ratios of ingredients needed to achieve this, while leaving a little room for your own improvisation.

In writing this book, we discovered that homemade ice cream, when served to guests, can be more impressive than the fanciest cakes and tarts. Its appeal is universal, and it delights all ages and at all life stages. Kids are fascinated by the process of making homemade ice cream, and unlike other forms of cooking, in which sharp knives and hot stoves are a constant worry, managing an ice cream recipe is a relatively simple, anxiety-free task that kids and adults can share. After all, the ingredients are few, the cooking steps are straightforward and the end result is quickly achieved. We hope you and your family and friends will enjoy these recipes and that they'll give you the foundation and confidence to go on and create more of your own delicious flavors. Enjoy.

— Marilyn and Tanya Linton

❧ The History of Ice Cream

If one of the measures of a food's success is its ability to go the distance, then ice cream has certainly passed the test of time. Just how far back it goes, no one really knows because much of the early history of ice cream remains unproven folklore. Though there are references that its beginnings may have reached as far back as ancient China, Persia and India, it's likely that ice cream evolved over centuries rather than having been invented on any particular day in any particular year. For instance, the Roman emperor Nero Claudius Caesar, who is said to have had an occasional craving for honey-flavored fruit-studded snow, sent his slaves into the mountains for the main ingredient.

In the 7th century, there are records of a Persian favorite: fruit-flavored crushed ice, known as *sharbat*, which was obviously a precursor to today's sherbet and not unlike the snow cones or flavored slushy refreshers typical of most modern fairgrounds. It's even likely that this sharbat was similar to a recipe the famed explorer Marco Polo is supposed to have brought back to Italy from China — if indeed he really did, for this may well be part of ice cream folklore. In ancient Greece and Turkey, concoctions similar to sharbat were also apparently enjoyed.

It is the Italians, however, who are credited with introducing ice cream to the rest of Europe. According to popular accounts, Catherine de' Medici, a Florentine who married Henry II of France in the mid-1500s, had her Italian chef make a variety of iced desserts — frozen thanks to icehouses, which were storage spaces (sometimes crude pits) for ice that was harvested. Part of the rich folklore surrounding ice cream also refers to an Italian chef who introduced ice cream to the British court.

In 1686, gelato (the Italian version of what in North America we call ice cream) found commercial success thanks to Sicilian Francesco Procopio dei Coltelli, who established Café Procope — a Parisian shrine to ice cream and coffee. In the United States, Dolley Madison, wife of President James Madison, is said to have served ice cream at her husband's inaugural ball. By the late 1800s, a recipe for homemade ice cream was published in an Italian cookbook: "Fill a bucket with crushed ice and salt. Set a second metal bucket with the ingredients in it and churn the ingredients vigorously for about an hour or until the mixture is creamy and smooth." In 1885, an Englishwoman, Agnes Marshall, wrote a whole book dedicated to ice cream.

❧ Ice Cream Makers

Chill and stir: then, as now, these were the basic instructions for making ice cream. Today, nothing much has changed except that an electric machine can do the work instead of your arm, churning the mixture as it freezes and incorporating air into it. You can make ice cream in the freezer, using a metal cake pan, but the resulting texture is closer to that of frozen cream (tasty enough but not as appealing in its mouth feel). Scientists have also demonstrated that adding liquid nitrogen to flavored cream instantly produces ice cream, but this party trick is worth avoiding, since liquid nitrogen can burn exposed skin.

Price is certainly a factor to consider when purchasing an ice cream maker, but it's worth remembering that the easier the machine is to use and the faster it produces results, the more you will use it. Every machine has the basics: a bowl, a dasher (its churning paddles) and a freezing mechanism. There are basically four different kinds of units.

Built-in compressor units

These top-of-the-line machines have their own built-in sealed fluorocarbon refrigerant systems. You put the chilled mixture into the machine's bowl, press the Chill and Churn buttons and, about 20 minutes later, are rewarded with supreme ice cream. These machines can churn out batches quickly, one after the other. Brand names to consider include Il Gelataio Magnum by Simac, the Robot Coupe Piccolo and Lussino (manufactured in Italy by Musso). These workhorses, most of which yield about 1 to 1½ quarts (1 to 1.5 L) of ice cream, take up a little more counter space than other units but have removable canisters for easy washing. Though they make ice cream making truly effortless, their price tags (up to $800 each) are hefty.

Manual and electric canister units

These ice cream makers have removable canisters lined with sealed liquid refrigerant, which you prefreeze. When you're ready to make ice cream, you insert the frozen canister into the machine, pour in the mixture and either flip the Churn switch or hand-crank the mixture. Some models freeze better than others, but we found that the smooth, dense texture of the ice cream produced by most of these machines didn't suffer if the last hour or two of freezing was done in a refrigerator freezer. Models are available in 1-pint (500 mL) or 1-quart (1 L) sizes. Prices are well under $100 (the hand-crank models are the least expensive). The only downside is that, because the canister liners take about eight to 10 hours to freeze, you are limited if you want to make more than one batch a day. Brand names to look for include Cuisinart, Donvier, Krups and Rival.

Ice-and-rock-salt units

These old-fashioned ice cream makers (available in electric and hand-crank models) make airier ice cream because the churning process takes longer and incorporates more air into the mixture. Though not as readily available as canister units and not cheap (wooden ones cost over $150, but plastic versions are less), these units — especially the hand-cranked ones — provide an opportunity to closely observe the ice cream making process while illustrating the principle (somewhat like taking a boat instead of a plane overseas does) that not everything worth doing happens instantaneously. In these models, the combination of ice and salt is the freezing mechanism: salt interferes with ice crystallization and allows the temperature to drop below the freezing point of water. If you're using one of these units, a good ratio of salt to ice is 2 cups (500 mL) salt to 8 lbs (4 kg) ice cubes or crushed ice. Using more salt produces a coarser-textured ice cream, while using less salt and taking longer to churn makes for a silkier dessert. Machines vary in size. White Mountain is one brand name (for more information, contact them at 1-800-343-0065).

Refrigerator freezers

Making ice cream in a refrigerator's freezer compartment is called "still freezing." But to avoid a rock-hard, unpleasant texture, you should manually incorporate air into the mixture by beating it several times during the freezing period. There are two popular methods. The first is to place the mixture in a metal loaf pan or square metal baking pan, cover it with plastic wrap and place it in the freezer until it is solid (about one to two hours); then, break the frozen mixture into pieces, spoon them into a food processor fitted with a metal blade and process until the mixture is soft but not melted. Repeat the freezing and processing a couple more times. The second method is to freeze the mixture until the edges are firm but the center is semisoft, then beat it with an electric mixer at medium-high speed until it is soft but not melted. Repeat the freezing and beating process a couple more times.

⁂ Other Equipment

Colander: A large metal or plastic colander is suitable for washing soft fruits for these recipes.

Food processor: When it's necessary to purée fruit or combine ingredients very well before freezing, a food processor fitted with a metal blade works well.

Grater: For finely grated lime and lemon zest, we prefer to use a carpenter's rasp (now sold under the name "microplane grater" in kitchen stores) instead of a zester or traditional grater.

Saucepan: A medium-size heavy-bottomed saucepan, preferably nonstick, is all that's needed for most recipes that require you to cook the ice cream mixture.

Sieve: A medium-size nylon sieve or fine-mesh strainer is great for straining custards and removing seeds from berry mixtures.

Spatula: Many ice cream makers come with a plastic spatula-scoop that fits the curve of the machine's canister perfectly. A selection of spatulas will come in handy for scooping, scraping and spreading.

Spoons: Heatproof plastic spoons are preferable because they're unlikely to retain flavors, as wooden spoons can.

Storage containers: Storage containers in several sizes are available in supermarkets and hardware stores. We prefer solid plastic containers not unlike those used for take-out foods or yogurt.

Whisks: Wire whisks in different sizes are handy for stirring custards and combining fruit mixtures.

❧ Perfect Scoops

You can get by with a sturdy tablespoon to scoop your ice cream at serving time, but a good ice cream scoop is worth the investment. Today, there are many styles to choose from. For sheer strength, we like the classic half-moon-shaped stainless-steel scoop. But visit any kitchen store and you will see much more variety — everything from simple metal spoon-shaped scoops with metal handles to easy-grip molded plastic scoops, some with quick-release levers built right in. The latest design has a nonstick, self-defrosting coating, which responds to the heat from your hand. For removing ice cream from the machine, we prefer a nonstick spade with a flat paddle-type head; this utensil is terrific for spreading and smoothing, as well. The trick to serving perfect scoops of ice cream that's a little hard is to first dip the scoop into hot water, then wipe it dry and quickly dip it into the ice cream. If you don't wipe it first, your scoop will be watery.

While serving the recipes in this book, we discovered that melon ballers are terrific tools, because we were often tasting many different preparations and wanted only a tiny scoop of each. Available from pea to grape size, melon ballers are also suitable for dinner-party desserts (guests may prefer a selection of miniature scoops instead of ice cream cone–size ones).

❧ Types of Ice Cream

Is it gelato or ice cream, granita or ice? There's a lot of confusion surrounding these simple concoctions. In our research, we found the following definitions to be consistent.

Ice cream

A creamy confection made from some combination of creams (as in heavy and light) or a combination of cream and whole milk, with or without eggs cooked into the mixture. A person's ice cream preference usually falls into either the egg-cream or all-cream (Philadelphia-style) category. As coauthors, we're split fifty-fifty.

Ice milk

A lightened-up version of ice cream made from whole or partly skimmed milk (skim milk produces a too-thin taste), without eggs.

Sherbet

A frozen dessert usually made from fruit purée and milk.

Gelato

The word, derived from the Italian verb *gelare* (to freeze), is used for both ice cream and ice milk but is generally less than 7% butterfat; one popular gelato formula calls for a combination of 10% whipping cream and 90% whole milk. Most gelatos contain 50% less air than most commercial ice creams, which gives them a smoother, denser texture.

Granita

These Italian-style water-based dairy-free ices are generally made with sugar syrup and flavored with fruit juices, coffee, tea or herbs and have a snowlike texture (granita is from the Italian word for "grain"). Granitas are made using the still-freezing method, which requires that the mixture be stirred several times during freezing to create the proper ice crystals.

Ice

A blend of puréed fruit or vegetables with water or sugar syrup, frozen by machine to a smooth texture. Figure on using 5 cups (1.25 L) of berries or fruit to produce about 2 cups (500 mL) of purée.

❧ Fat Content

Regular ice cream

To be called ice cream, a product must have a butterfat content of at least 10%.

Low-fat

Low-fat usually means 3 grams of fat or less per serving.

Light

This term often means that the product contains 50% less fat than the same brand's regular ice cream.

Non-fat

For a product to be non-fat, it must contain less than 0.5 grams of fat per serving.

❧ A Lot of Air

Air is incorporated into ice cream during the freezing process; the amount of air incorporated is called "overrun" in commercial ice cream. Without it, ice cream would be nothing but a frozen brick. Commercial overrun percentages can range from 21% to close to 100%. Low overrun produces denser, creamier ice cream and is what you're likely to get with your home ice cream maker. High overrun results in a product that is very light and pillowy and melts quite quickly. In addition to air, commercially made ice cream contains emulsifiers, such as mono- and diglycerides, to prevent the fat from separating from the ice cream mass. Carob, carrageenan and guar gum are all popular stabilizers used to prevent the formation of ice crystals in low-fat mixtures and protect against heat shock caused by changes in temperature that take place in transit.

❧ Ingredients

As with all cooking-from-scratch recipes, we use only the freshest and finest ingredients. Here are the most common.

Simple syrup: This is the basis for many of our ices, sherbets, gelatos and ice creams. This sugar syrup is a combination of one part sugar to one part water that's heated until the sugar dissolves, then cooled. You can make it in large batches and store it in the refrigerator for up to three months so it's ready when needed (see recipe, page 20).

Corn syrup: Used in some recipes as a sweetener, it helps create a light, smooth texture.

Cream

Whipping (35%) cream: Sometimes called heavy cream, this full-fat cream is essential on its own or in combination with a lower-fat cream, such as half-and-half, or milk to make ice cream. Though ice cream can be made by adding whipped cream to the final churnings of the remaining ingredients, we prefer to add it in its liquid state.

Table (18%) cream: This cream, commonly used in coffee, is lower in fat than whipping cream and is used extensively in ice cream making.

Half-and-half (10%) cream: This mixture of milk and cream is a good substitute for table cream in recipes.

Sour cream: Its slightly tart flavor and smooth texture are nice paired with many fruits, especially blueberries, and make rich ice cream. Though sour cream is now available in reduced-fat and non-fat varieties, the best ice cream uses the full-fat version.

Milk

Whole milk: We prefer whole homogenized milk (3.3% fat), though reduced-fat (2%) works well, especially when combined with whole milk or light cream. Avoid 1% or skim milk, as they deliver very little taste when frozen. Lactose-free milk can be substituted.

Non-fat powdered milk: Though not an ingredient used in most kitchens, powdered milk is economical and needs no refrigeration until it is reconstituted with water.

Evaporated milk: Available in cans, evaporated milk is more concentrated than whole milk; use it undiluted.

Sweetened condensed milk: Unlike evaporated milk, this is concentrated milk with a large amount of added sugar; when called for, use it undiluted.

Yogurt: Milk that has fermented and coagulated through the addition of beneficial bacteria, yogurt comes in plain, flavored, low-fat and fat-free varieties. The higher the fat, the more stable the product.

Goat's milk: Goat's milk makes an interesting ice cream with a distinctive taste that's not unlike that of goat cheese. Try it paired with honey or flavored with blueberries or dried cranberries.

Soy beverage: An alternative for anyone who dislikes or is allergic to dairy, soy beverages come sweetened or unsweetened, plain or flavored.

Coconut milk: Used today to add an Asian or Caribbean flavor to food, canned coconut milk is a liquid made from the flesh of the coconut.

Cheeses: Low-fat fromage frais is fresh white cheese made with whole or skim milk and cream. It has the consistency of cream cheese, with fewer calories and less cholesterol, and is terrific when added to fruit-based ice creams. The soft, creamy texture of ricotta and the richness of mascarpone also provide excellent flavor. Cheeses are best added to ice cream that is semifrozen, because their high fat content can make the ice cream too buttery if they're churned too long.

Other Ingredients

Eggs: We use large eggs. Egg safety: Use only fresh eggs that have been stored in the refrigerator. If you find a cracked egg in the carton, throw it out. In the egg-based ice creams in this book, we suggest you cook the eggs together with the milk or cream to at least 160°F (70°C). Though the risk of salmonella in uncooked eggs is low, the illness is a serious one. Better to be safe than sorry.

Gelatin: We add gelatin to some recipes to help create a smooth texture.

Chocolate: Throughout this book, we suggest you buy good-quality chocolate for your ices and ice cream mixtures. Here are some things to consider.

- Buy chocolate from a retailer whose products turn over quickly and don't sit on the shelf. Make sure that the chocolate package looks new and not dusty.
- Old chocolate can look pale and powdery (this is called bloom) because of being stored in an overly warm place. You can still use it. The flavor and texture are only slightly changed.
- Bittersweet chocolate is made from chocolate liquor sweetened with sugar and is blended with additional cocoa butter. Look for chocolate with at least 35% chocolate liquor.

❧ Quantity

Each recipe in this book makes about 1 quart (1 L). However, because ice cream makers incorporate different amounts of air, and so many other factors, including the freezing method and the temperature of the ingredients prior to freezing, affect the final yield, you may get a little more or a little less with each recipe. Generally speaking, 1 quart (1 L) is enough for six adults.

❧ Hygiene and Food Safety

Ice cream makers and any utensils used during the process of making ice cream or ices should be kept scrupulously clean by washing in hot soapy water and rinsing in hot water. All dairy ingredients should be cold. When making an egg custard as an ice cream base, we recommend that you cook the custard to 185°F (85°C) to kill bacteria. It's important to keep stirring the custard to ensure that the eggs don't curdle, but if they do, a good remedy is to strain the custard through a fine sieve when you have finished cooking it.

Every cooked custard must be cooled before it can be transferred to an ice cream maker. To minimize the potential for bacterial growth, put the pan containing the hot custard into a bowl of ice water and stir it occasionally until it's room temperature and cool enough to refrigerate.

To further minimize the risk of illness, we recommend using powdered egg whites instead of fresh ones when egg whites are called for.

❦ Storage

Store each batch in a freezerproof container (we found that most plastic take-out tubs work just fine) in the main part of your freezer, not on your freezer door. Commercially, ice cream is stored at three different temperatures: The deep freeze (−15 to −22°F/−26 to −30°C) is used when the product is first made. In its distribution phase and for supermarket storage, the temperature is −4°F (−20°C) or less. In the display case, from which your ice cream is usually served at an ice cream shop, the storage is a little warmer (about 4 to 7°F/−16 to −14°C) so the ice cream can be scooped easily. To make ice cream at home, you should be able to get the temperature to 18 to 21°F (−8 to −6°C) in the machine, then harden it in your home freezer, which is usually in the −4°F (−20°C) range.

When filling a plastic tub with ice cream, leave about ¼ inch (0.5 cm) headspace to allow for any increase in volume that occurs during the freezing process. Also, place a piece of plastic wrap on top of the ice cream before putting the lid of the tub on; this provides an excellent seal against any moisture and keeps the surface from drying out.

❦ How Much Alcohol?

Using too much alcohol in a recipe prevents ice cream or ices from freezing well. Use the following as your guide: for 4 cups (1 L) base mixture, use less than 1 cup (250 mL) wine of up to 12% alcohol, up to ½ cup (125 mL) dessert wine or liqueur of up to 25% alcohol, or up to ¼ cup (50 mL) distilled alcohol of up to 48% alcohol.

❧ Perfect Ice Cream

We evaluate ice cream, like wine, according to certain criteria, including appearance, texture, flavor and meltability.

Appearance is the most obvious, and it's undoubtedly an important attribute when you consider the role your eyes play in choosing one ice cream over another among tubs on display in an ice cream shop. A good ice cream is devoid of ice crystals and has no evidence of shrinkage from the sides of its container. Any nuts, raisins or candies mixed in should be evenly distributed. The color is less important; for instance, some people like pistachio ice cream a pale natural green, while others like the neon color that results from the addition of green food coloring.

The texture of an ice cream or an ice should be smooth. Visible ice crystals indicate that the ice cream is too old, has been poorly mixed or contains the wrong ratio of ingredients.

We think the flavor should be true to itself. Strawberry should taste like the real berry, chocolate should be made from the finest chocolate. The balance is important: some ice creams are overpowering in their flavor, and the pleasure of wanting more than a spoonful or two is therefore denied. On the other hand, some flavors are so limp and weak that virtually all you can taste is the frozen milk or cream. We find that the acceptability of sweetness is subjective, but ice cream or ices that are overly sweet can obliterate any flavor, which is truly unfortunate.

Finally, meltability is important. One of our failures (the recipe was obviously scrapped) was an ice cream that remained rock-solid despite standing for 10 minutes at room temperature. Ice cream should melt to a creamy puddle, an ice to a pool of flavored water.

❧ Why Your Ice Cream Won't Freeze and Other Problems

When your ice cream finishes in a semifrozen, not frozen, state.
Many home ice cream makers produce softer ice cream than is found in commercial products — and many people prefer their ice cream this way. To harden, or "ripen," an ice cream before serving, transfer it from the machine to a freezerproof container, then place it in the freezer until it achieves the consistency you prefer.

When your ice cream has large ice crystals.
If the temperature of the prepared ingredients was below 40°F (5°C) when the freezing began, the mixture may have frozen too fast and not allowed the machine to incorporate enough air.

When your ice cream has hardened in the freezer to a rock-solid mass. Because homemade ice creams contain no commercial stabilizers, they will freeze harder even though they may have been soft straight out of the machine. Check the firmness of your ice cream an hour before serving time. If it's rock-solid, temper it by placing it in the refrigerator for 10 to 15 minutes. To soften ice cream even faster, spoon it into the bowl of a food processor fitted with a metal blade and whirl it until it is smooth but not melted. Or beat it with an electric mixer until soft.

TOP LICKS

In 2001, the Top 5 flavors of ice cream in the United States were vanilla, chocolate, Neapolitan, butter pecan and chocolate chip.

Simple Syrup

MAKES 3 CUPS (750 mL)

Tip: The reduced-sugar version will produce a firmer texture when added to ices and sorbets and then frozen. Recipes made with this version are best served right away, softened slightly before scooping or scraped into a shaved granita-style dessert.

This recipe is the basis of many of the frozen desserts in this book. It's easy to make, and you can cover and keep it in the refrigerator for up to three months. We also use it to sweeten iced tea, limeade and lemonade. For a less sweet version, decrease the sugar to 1 cup (250 mL); see Tip, left. Double the recipe to make a larger quantity if you plan to make lots of ice cream or ices in the next couple of months.

| 2 cups | granulated sugar | 500 mL |
| 2 cups | water | 500 mL |

1. In a medium saucepan over medium-low heat, bring sugar and water to a simmer. Cook, stirring, for 1 minute or until sugar is completely dissolved. Simmer, without stirring, for 2 minutes more.

2. Transfer to an airtight container and refrigerate until cold.

Chocolatey Ice Creams

Classic Chocolate Ice Cream

Everybody needs a basic recipe for chocolate ice cream, which is one of the five most popular flavors in North America. This one is simple but does the trick. A couple of scoops make the perfect dessert. To make it even more decadent, add a chocolate sauce topping or a sprinkle of chocolate nuts or chopped nuts.

Tip: Melting chocolate is very easy but requires close attention because it can burn quickly. Our method is to melt it in the top half of a double boiler over simmering water. If you don't have a double boiler, use a saucepan and a stainless-steel bowl. Pour in enough water to come 1 inch (2.5 cm) up side of saucepan. Bring to a simmer over medium heat. Place chocolate in bowl. Place over pan and stir until melted.

• Double boiler

6 oz	bittersweet chocolate, coarsely chopped	175 g
¼ cup	unsweetened cocoa powder	50 mL
4	egg yolks	4
¾ cup	granulated sugar	175 mL
2 cups	whipping (35%) cream	500 mL
2 cups	milk	500 mL
1 tsp	vanilla	5 mL

1. In the top of a double boiler over medium heat, melt chocolate (see Tip, left). Gradually whisk in cocoa until smooth. Set aside.

2. In a bowl, whisk egg yolks with sugar until thickened and pale yellow. Set aside.

3. In a medium saucepan over medium-low heat, bring cream and milk to a simmer. Gradually whisk into the egg mixture.

4. Return the entire mixture to the saucepan. Cook over low heat, stirring constantly, until the mixture is thick enough to coat the back of a wooden spoon. Be careful not to let it boil. Strain into a clean large bowl. Let cool to room temperature.

5. Stir in melted chocolate and vanilla. Cover and refrigerate until completely cold or overnight.

6. Stir cream mixture. Transfer to an ice cream maker and freeze according to manufacturer's instructions.

Neapolitan Ice Cream

Bricks of chocolate, strawberry and vanilla ice cream are known as Neapolitan and are easy to make at home. You can layer homemade ice cream immediately after it's finished churning or you can soften already frozen homemade or store-bought ice cream, layer it, then refreeze it until it's solid.

- 9- by 5-inch (1.5 L) loaf pan, lined with plastic wrap or waxed paper

2 cups	chocolate ice cream	500 mL
2 cups	strawberry ice cream	500 mL
2 cups	vanilla ice cream	500 mL

1. Soften chocolate ice cream at room temperature for 15 minutes. Spread softened ice cream in prepared pan. Smooth top with a spatula. Freeze until firm.

2. Soften strawberry ice cream at room temperature for 15 minutes. Spread softened ice cream over first layer. Smooth top with a spatula. Freeze until firm.

3. Soften vanilla ice cream at room temperature for 15 minutes. Spread softened ice cream over second layer. Smooth top with a spatula. Cover with plastic wrap or waxed paper and freeze for 4 hours or until firm.

4. To serve, unwrap and turn out of pan onto cutting board. Peel off plastic wrap. Using a warm dry knife, cut into slices or scoop into sundaes drizzled with chocolate sauce.

SERVES 6 TO 8

The Ultimate Chocolate Ice Cream

There are two reasons this is the best. The first is that we use chocolate that is 70% cocoa; the second is that the base we use is a rich caramel custard. The result is a chocolate ice cream with an unforgettable intensity. It's worth the extra work, so try it!

Tip: Double-intensity vanilla packs twice the flavor and aromatic richness of ordinary vanilla, but without extra sugar. It can be purchased at gourmet stores. If you can't find it, use ½ tsp (2 mL) regular vanilla.

1 cup	milk	250 mL
1 cup	whipping (35%) cream	250 mL
½ tsp	double-intensity vanilla	2 mL
½ cup + 5 tbsp	granulated sugar, divided	200 mL
⅓ cup	water	75 mL
6	egg yolks	6
Pinch	salt	Pinch
2	bars (each 3½ oz/100 g) 70% cocoa dark chocolate, finely chopped	2

1. In a medium saucepan, bring milk, cream and vanilla to a boil over low heat, stirring constantly. Remove from heat and set aside.

2. In a large saucepan, combine the ½ cup (125 mL) sugar and the water; bring to a boil over medium heat, stirring until sugar is dissolved. Boil until mixture turns a deep caramel color, 7 to 10 minutes. Remove from heat and carefully and gradually whisk in the warm milk mixture, taking care not to burn yourself, as the mixture sizzles and steams. Set aside.

3. In a medium bowl, using an electric mixer, beat egg yolks until tripled in volume. Mix in the remaining 5 tbsp (75 mL) sugar and the salt. Slowly add the hot caramel mixture, mixing on low until well combined. Return to saucepan and cook over low heat, stirring constantly, until caramel custard has thickened enough to coat the back of a spoon.

4. Place chocolate in a large bowl. Press custard through a fine sieve into the bowl of chocolate and whisk until melted and smooth. Let cool to room temperature. Cover and refrigerate until completely cold or overnight.

5. Stir cream mixture. Transfer to an ice cream maker and freeze according to manufacturer's instructions.

Chocolate Mousse Ice Cream

SERVES 6 TO 8

This ice cream tastes like frozen chocolate mousse. Unlike the classic French dessert, this treat has no eggs, just loads of bittersweet chocolate. Use the best-quality chocolate you can find. It will definitely make a difference!

12 oz	bittersweet chocolate, chopped	375 g
2 cups	milk	500 mL
2 cups	whipping (35%) cream	500 mL
½ cup	granulated sugar	125 mL
1 tbsp	vanilla	15 mL

1. Place chocolate in a bowl. In a medium saucepan over medium-low heat, bring milk, cream and sugar to a simmer, stirring occasionally. Gradually whisk into chocolate until smooth. Whisk in vanilla.

2. Cover and refrigerate until completely cold or overnight.

3. Stir cream mixture. Transfer to an ice cream maker and freeze according to manufacturer's instructions.

Hot Chocolate Ice Cream

No, it's not really hot, but it is made with hot chocolate mix! This recipe is super-simple and really flavorful. To make it truly authentic, top with marshmallows and shaved chocolate.

Tip: Egg safety: Use only fresh eggs that have been stored in the refrigerator. If you find a cracked egg in the carton, throw it out. In the egg-based ice creams in this book , we suggest that you cook the eggs together with the milk or cream to at least 160°F (70°C). Though the risk of salmonella in uncooked eggs is low, the illness is a serious one. Better to be safe than sorry.

3	egg yolks	3
1/2 cup	granulated sugar	125 mL
4	packages (1 oz/28 g) hot chocolate mix	4
2 cups	milk	500 mL
2 cups	whipping (35%) cream	500 mL

1. In a bowl, whisk egg yolks with sugar until thickened and pale yellow. Set aside.

2. In a medium saucepan over low heat, whisk chocolate mix into milk and bring to a simmer. Gradually whisk into the egg mixture.

3. Return entire mixture to the saucepan. Cook over low heat, stirring constantly, until the mixture is thick enough to coat the back of a wooden spoon. Be careful not to let it boil. Strain into a clean large bowl. Let cool to room temperature.

4. Stir in whipping cream. Cover and refrigerate until completely cold or overnight.

5. Stir cream mixture. Transfer to an ice cream maker and freeze according to manufacturer's instructions.

Mix-Ins

The sky's the limit when it comes to what you can add to basic ice cream flavors such as vanilla or chocolate. You can mix in anything from crushed cookies to smashed toffee in the last 5 minutes of freezing or you can smush your signature additions into store-bought or previously frozen homemade ice cream.

Here's our Top 20...

- diced dried apricots
- brownie pieces
- crumbled gingersnaps
- chocolate-covered espresso beans
- toasted flaked coconut
- M&M's
- Reese's Pieces
- Grape-Nuts
- granola
- semisweet and white chocolate chips
- chopped sponge toffee
- gummi bears
- toasted nuts
- chocolate sprinkles
- peanuts
- raisins
- red pepper flakes
- ground cinnamon
- chopped dates
- crushed peppermint candy canes

Fiery Chocolate Ice Cream

Areeeeba! This is one spicy chocolate ice cream! At first, it tastes like regular ice cream, and then the spice kicks in. If you're tired of plain old chocolate, this one offers a fresh twist.

Tip: Be careful not to pour the hot milk mixture into the egg mixture too quickly. You don't want to scramble the eggs.

3	egg yolks	3
¾ cup	granulated sugar	175 mL
2 cups	milk	500 mL
6 oz	bittersweet chocolate, coarsely chopped	175 g
¼ cup	unsweetened cocoa powder	50 mL
2 cups	whipping (35%) cream	500 mL
1	jalapeño pepper, seeded and finely chopped	1
1 tsp	vanilla	5 mL

1. In a bowl, whisk egg yolks with sugar until thickened and pale yellow. Set aside.

2. In a medium saucepan over low heat, bring milk, chocolate and cocoa powder to a simmer. Gradually whisk into the egg mixture.

3. Return entire mixture to the saucepan. Cook over low heat, stirring constantly, until the mixture is thick enough to coat the back of a wooden spoon. Be careful not to let it boil. Strain into a clean large bowl. Let cool to room temperature.

4. Stir in whipping cream, jalapeño and vanilla. Cover and refrigerate until completely cold or overnight.

5. Stir cream mixture. Transfer to an ice cream maker and freeze according to manufacturer's instructions.

Chocolate Banana Cinnamon Ice Cream

SERVES 8 TO 10

Few things go better together than chocolate and bananas, so we made an ice cream out of the delicious duo. After testing it, though, we felt it could use an extra kick, so we added cinnamon. The result was fabulous!

3	egg yolks	3
¾ cup	granulated sugar	175 mL
8 oz	unsweetened chocolate, finely chopped	250 g
2 cups	milk	500 mL
3	ripe, mushy bananas (about 2 cups/500 mL)	3
2 tbsp	ground cinnamon	25 mL
2 cups	whipping (35%) cream	500 mL

1. In a bowl, whisk egg yolks with sugar until thickened and pale yellow. Set aside.

2. In a medium saucepan, combine chocolate and milk. Cook over low heat, stirring occasionally, until chocolate is melted. Increase heat to medium-low. Bring to a simmer. Cook, stirring constantly, for 1 minute to combine. Gradually whisk into the egg mixture.

3. Return entire mixture to the saucepan. Cook over low heat, stirring constantly, until the mixture is thick enough to coat the back of a wooden spoon. Be careful not to let it boil. Strain into a clean large bowl. Let cool to room temperature.

4. Mash the bananas with the cinnamon. Add to the custard mixture, along with the whipping cream; mix well. Cover and refrigerate until completely cold or overnight.

5. Stir cream mixture. Transfer to an ice cream maker and freeze according to manufacturer's instructions.

Chocolate Hazelnut Ice Cream

30   CHOCOLATEY ICE CREAMS

SERVES 8

Ever wondered what else you could do with chocolate hazelnut spread other than put it on toast? We melted it into ice cream and found the result delicious. This spread gives the ice cream a pleasantly grainy, slightly chewy texture.

Tip: If you prefer just a hint of hazelnut flavor, reduce the chocolate hazelnut spread to ½ cup (125 mL).

Serving suggestion: Splash your scoop with your favorite hazelnut liqueur.

2 cups	whipping (35%) cream	500 mL
2 cups	milk	500 mL
1 cup	chocolate hazelnut spread (see Tip, left)	250 mL
½ cup	granulated sugar	125 mL
¼ cup	chopped hazelnuts	50 mL

1. In a medium saucepan over medium-low heat, bring cream and milk to a simmer.

2. In a large bowl, stir hazelnut spread with sugar until smooth. Whisk ¼ cup (50 mL) of the cream mixture into the sugar mixture until smooth. Whisk in remaining cream mixture until blended. Cover and refrigerate until completely cold or overnight.

3. Stir cream mixture. Transfer to an ice cream maker and freeze according to manufacturer's instructions.

4. Serve sprinkled with chopped hazelnuts.

Variation

Double Chocolate Hazelnut Ice Cream: If you really love chocolate, add ½ cup (125 mL) chopped good-quality dark chocolate and the hazelnuts a few seconds before the ice cream churning has finished.

Chocolate Malt Ice Cream

This very rich ice cream, reminiscent of those at a '40s malt shop, is chocolatey but not too sweet. You can find malted milk powder in most large supermarkets in the same section as hot chocolate powders.

Tip: This ice cream will be soft. For firmer ice cream, place in the freezer for at least 2 hours.

2	eggs	2
4 oz	unsweetened chocolate, chopped	125 g
2 cups	table (18%) cream	500 mL
¾ cup	granulated sugar	175 mL
⅓ cup	malted milk powder	75 mL
1 cup	whipping (35%) cream	250 mL
2 tsp	vanilla	10 mL

1. In a bowl, whisk eggs until pale yellow. Set aside.

2. In a medium saucepan, combine chocolate, table cream, sugar and malted milk powder. Cook over low heat, stirring occasionally, until chocolate is melted and sugar is dissolved. Increase heat to medium-low. Bring to a simmer. Cook, stirring constantly, for 1 minute to combine. Gradually whisk into the eggs.

3. Return entire mixture to the saucepan. Cook over low heat, stirring constantly, until the mixture is thick enough to coat the back of a wooden spoon. Be careful not to let it boil. Strain into a clean large bowl. Let cool to room temperature.

4. Stir in whipping cream and vanilla. Cover and refrigerate until completely cold or overnight.

5. Stir cream mixture. Transfer to an ice cream maker and freeze according to manufacturer's instructions.

Chocolate Meringue Plates

Many ice cream recipes call for just egg yolks, so this is a great way to use some of the extra egg whites. This will make a crisp meringue with a good chocolate punch. Put one of these discs on a plate and top it with your favorite ice cream and a bit of fresh fruit. Or crumble it on top of ice cream for a delicious fat-free topping.

- Preheat oven to 200°F (100°C) and place racks in the top third and bottom third of oven
- 2 baking sheets, lined with parchment paper

10½ tbsp	granulated sugar, divided	157 mL
½ cup	confectioner's (icing) sugar	125 mL
3 tbsp	unsweetened cocoa powder	45 mL
4	egg whites	4

1. Using a cereal bowl or a container, trace four 4-inch (10 cm) circles on each sheet of parchment paper, spaced about 1 inch (2.5 cm) apart. Turn papers over (you should be able to see the circles through the paper).

2. In a medium bowl, sift together 3 tbsp (45 mL) of the granulated sugar, the confectioner's sugar and cocoa.

3. In a large bowl, using an electric mixer with whisk attachment, beat egg whites until frothy. Add 1½ tbsp (22 mL) of the granulated sugar and beat until soft peaks form. Gradually add the remaining 6 tbsp (75 mL) sugar. Continue beating until whites are stiff and glossy. Fold in cocoa mixture, being careful not to overmix.

4. Using a $^1\!/_2$-cup (125 mL) measure, scoop meringue into the centers of the circles. Using the back of a spoon, carefully spread to the edges of the circles.

5. Bake in preheated oven for about 4 hours, rotating the position of the baking sheets every hour, until shiny and firm to the touch. Turn oven off and leave meringues in oven until cool or overnight.

Tip: Leave a sticky note on the oven door to let everyone know there are meringues cooling inside. Many meringues have become toasted when someone preheated the oven for another recipe!

❧ **MAKES 8 MERINGUES**

Chocolate Macaroon Ice Cream

Use sweetened coconut and the best-quality chocolate you can find. We promise, the ingredient hunting will be well worth it.

3	egg yolks	3
¾ cup	granulated sugar	175 mL
8 oz	unsweetened chocolate, finely chopped	250 g
2 cups	milk	500 mL
2 cups	whipping (35%) cream	500 mL
1 cup	sweetened shredded coconut	250 mL

1. In a bowl, whisk egg yolks with sugar until thickened and pale yellow. Set aside.

2. In a medium saucepan, combine chocolate and milk. Cook over low heat, stirring occasionally, until chocolate is melted. Increase heat to medium-low. Bring to a simmer. Cook, stirring constantly, for 1 minute to combine. Gradually whisk into the egg mixture.

3. Return entire mixture to the saucepan. Cook over low heat, stirring constantly, until the mixture is thick enough to coat the back of a wooden spoon. Be careful not to let it boil. Strain into a clean large bowl. Let cool to room temperature.

4. Stir in whipping cream. Cover and refrigerate until completely cold or overnight.

5. Stir cream mixture. Transfer to an ice cream maker and freeze according to manufacturer's instructions. Add coconut in the last 5 minutes of freezing and let machine stir it in.

Black Forest Ice Cream

This ice cream has all the ingredients found in the classic cake: cherries, chocolate and whipped cream. To get the cake taste, we added chopped brownies. The secret is to add the cherries and brownies just before the freezing is over; otherwise, they sink to the bottom. The result is to die for.

Tip: Garnish with some shaved chocolate.

3	egg yolks	3
¾ cup	granulated sugar	175 mL
8 oz	unsweetened chocolate, finely chopped	250 g
2 cups	milk	500 mL
2 cups	whipping (35%) cream	500 mL
2 cups	chopped brownies (store-bought will do)	500 mL
1 cup	drained canned sour cherries	250 mL

1. In a bowl, whisk egg yolks with sugar until thickened and pale yellow. Set aside.

2. In a medium saucepan, combine chocolate and milk. Cook over low heat, stirring occasionally, until chocolate is melted. Increase heat to medium-low. Bring to a simmer. Cook, stirring constantly, for 1 minute to combine. Gradually whisk into the egg mixture.

3. Return entire mixture to the saucepan. Cook over low heat, stirring constantly, until the mixture is thick enough to coat the back of a wooden spoon. Be careful not to let it boil. Strain into a clean large bowl. Let cool to room temperature.

4. Stir in whipping cream. Cover and refrigerate until completely cold or overnight.

5. Stir cream mixture. Transfer to an ice cream maker and freeze according to manufacturer's instructions. Add brownies and cherries in the last 5 minutes of freezing and let machine stir them in.

Raspberry White Chocolate Ribbon Ice Cream

SERVES 8 TO 10

Raspberries and white chocolate are divine together.

Tips: You can use fresh raspberries if you prefer; just let them sit a bit longer so they release as much juice as possible.

Be careful not to pour the hot milk mixture into the egg mixture too quickly. You don't want to scramble the eggs.

Don't cook your egg mixture over too high a heat or the eggs will scramble. If they do scramble, strain the mixture through a fine sieve.

4 cups	frozen raspberries	1 L
1 1/2 cups	granulated sugar, divided	375 mL
	Juice of 1/2 lemon	
2	eggs	2
2 cups	whipping (35%) cream	500 mL
1 cup	milk	250 mL
4 oz	white chocolate, coarsely chopped	125 g

White Chocolate Ribbon

1/2 cup	whipping (35%) cream	125 mL
4 oz	white chocolate, chopped	125 g

1. In a bowl, combine raspberries, 3/4 cup (175 mL) of the sugar and lemon juice. Let stand for 1 hour, stirring every 15 minutes.

2. In another bowl, whisk eggs with the remaining 3/4 cup (175 mL) sugar until thickened and pale yellow. Set aside.

3. In a medium saucepan over medium-low heat, bring cream and milk to a simmer. Gradually whisk into the egg mixture.

4. Return entire mixture to the saucepan. Cook over low heat, stirring constantly, until the mixture is thick enough to coat the back of a wooden spoon. Be careful not to let it boil. Strain into a clean large bowl.

5. Mash raspberries with the back of a spoon to release juice. Stir into cream mixture. Let cool to room temperature. Cover and refrigerate until completely cold or overnight.

6. Stir cream mixture. Transfer to an ice cream maker and freeze according to manufacturer's instructions. Add white chocolate in the last 5 minutes of freezing and let machine stir it in.

7. *To make White Chocolate Ribbon:* In a double boiler over medium heat, combine cream and white chocolate. Cook, stirring, until chocolate is melted. Let cool completely.

8. In a freezerproof container, alternate layers of ice cream and white chocolate ribbon, making about 3 layers of each. Using a knife, gently swirl the mixture. Cover and freeze until firm.

White Chocolate Ice Cream

White chocolate seems like an extravagant ingredient in ice cream, but everyone enjoys a little indulgence now and then. This is a simple and elegant ice cream that is bound to impress at the end of a formal dinner. Rest assured, however, that it's as binge-worthy as many others. Because of its rich flavor, this dessert requires no eggs to thicken it or to add texture.

Serving suggestions: Serve with fresh raspberries, blueberries or strawberries.

2 cups	whipping (35%) cream	500 mL
2 cups	milk	500 mL
1/3 cup	granulated sugar	75 mL
8 oz	white chocolate, coarsely chopped	250 g
2 tsp	vanilla	10 mL

1. In a medium saucepan over medium-low heat, bring cream, milk and sugar to a simmer.

2. Place white chocolate in a bowl. Pour cream mixture over top and let stand for 5 minutes. Whisk until smooth. Whisk in vanilla.

3. Cover and refrigerate until completely cold or overnight.

4. Stir cream mixture. Transfer to an ice cream maker and freeze according to manufacturer's instructions.

❧ Variations

White Chocolate Cranberry Pistachio Ice Cream: Add 1/4 cup (50 mL) dried cranberries and 1/4 cup (50 mL) chopped raw unsalted pistachios in the last 5 minutes of freezing and let machine stir them in.

White Chocolate Ginger Ice Cream: Add 1/4 cup (50 mL) finely chopped crystallized ginger in the last 5 minutes of freezing and let machine stir it in.

Sugar & Spice Ice Creams

Old-Fashioned Vanilla Ice Cream

Any ice cream book just has to contain a recipe for vanilla ice cream, which, though basic, is a favorite and therefore never ordinary. It really doesn't get much better than this.

Serving suggestion:
Ice Cream Sandwiches: Sandwich one generous scoop of softened Old-Fashioned Vanilla Ice Cream between two chocolate-covered digestive cookies. Gently press to squish ice cream to the edges of the cookies. Using a knife, smooth sides. To decorate, spread chocolate sprinkles, toasted coconut, mini chocolate chips or crushed nuts on a flat plate. Firmly press the edges of the sandwich into the topping. Place on a baking sheet and freeze until firm.

4	egg yolks	4
3/4 cup	granulated sugar	175 mL
1	vanilla bean	1
2 cups	milk	500 mL
2 cups	whipping (35%) cream	500 mL

1. In a bowl, whisk egg yolks with sugar until thickened and pale yellow. Set aside.

2. Slit vanilla bean lengthwise and scrape seeds into a medium saucepan. Add vanilla pod, milk and cream. Place saucepan over medium-low heat and bring to a simmer. Remove from heat. Let stand for 15 minutes, allowing the flavor of the vanilla to infuse.

3. Discard pod. Bring mixture to a simmer over low heat and simmer for 5 minutes. Gradually whisk into the egg mixture.

4. Return entire mixture to the saucepan. Cook over low heat, stirring constantly, until the mixture is thick enough to coat the back of a wooden spoon. Be careful not to let it boil. Strain into a clean large bowl. Let cool to room temperature. Cover and refrigerate until completely cold or overnight.

5. Stir cream mixture. Transfer to an ice cream maker and freeze according to manufacturer's instructions.

❧ Variation

Saffron Ice Cream: Stir a pinch of saffron threads into the strained cream mixture before refrigerating.

Baked Alaska

Transform Old-Fashioned Vanilla Ice Cream into individual servings of baked Alaska for a special party. Make sure the ice cream is very firm before slathering on the meringue. The egg whites are not fully cooked; because of today's concern over salmonella, we prefer to substitute pasteurized powdered egg whites or egg whites in a carton for fresh.

- **Preheat oven to 450°F (230°C)**
- **Baking sheet, lined with parchment paper**

6	flat cookies, about 2 inches (5 cm) in diameter	6
6	scoops Old-Fashioned Vanilla Ice Cream	6
4	egg whites or ½ cup (125 mL) liquid pasteurized egg whites (see Tip, below)	4
¼ tsp	cream of tartar	1 mL
¾ cup	granulated sugar	175 mL

1. Place cookies on prepared baking sheet. Top each with one scoop ice cream. Freeze for 1 hour or until hard.

2. Meanwhile, in a bowl, beat egg whites until foamy. Add cream of tartar and beat until soft peaks form.

3. Gradually add sugar. Continue to beat until stiff glossy peaks form.

4. Remove the ice cream and cookies from the freezer. Using a spatula or spoon and working quickly, spread meringue completely over ice cream and cookies, making certain to cover all the ice cream right down to the cookie crust.

5. Bake in preheated oven until golden brown, about 6 minutes. Serve immediately.

Tip: ½ cup (125 mL) liquid pasteurized egg whites is equivalent to 4 fresh egg whites. Egg whites are now available in cartons in the supermarket dairy section. They're great to have on hand for egg white omelets (no cholesterol) or to make angel food cake.

❧ **SERVES 6**

Honey Vanilla Ice Cream

This was a favorite among our taste testers. It's especially enjoyable as is, but also makes a wonderful base for all sorts of additions, from crushed peanuts to chocolate chips to toasted coconut to chopped dates.

Tips: Be careful not to pour the hot milk mixture into the egg mixture too quickly. You don't want to scramble the eggs.

Don't cook your egg mixture over too high a heat or the eggs will scramble. If they do scramble, strain the mixture through a fine sieve.

4	egg yolks	4
1/2 cup	liquid honey	125 mL
1 cup	whipping (35%) cream	250 mL
1 cup	milk	250 mL
1 tbsp	vanilla	15 mL

1. In a bowl, whisk egg yolks with honey until thickened and pale yellow. Set aside.

2. In a medium saucepan over medium-low heat, bring cream and milk to a simmer. Gradually whisk into the egg mixture.

3. Return entire mixture to the saucepan. Cook over low heat, stirring constantly, until the mixture is thick enough to coat the back of a wooden spoon. Be careful not to let it boil. Strain into a clean large bowl. Let cool to room temperature.

4. Stir in vanilla. Cover and refrigerate until completely cold or overnight.

5. Stir cream mixture. Transfer to an ice cream maker and freeze according to manufacturer's instructions.

Tip: For extra richness, substitute the seeds from 1 vanilla bean for the vanilla extract. Slit vanilla bean lengthwise. Scrape seeds into a medium saucepan. Add vanilla pod, milk and cream. Bring to a simmer over medium-low heat. Proceed with recipe.

✂ Variations

Lavender Vanilla Ice Cream: This delicious treat is found throughout the south of France, where the flowering herb grows in every garden and at the sides of roads. Add 2 tbsp (25 mL) crushed dried lavender flowers to the strained cream mixture. When you buy lavender, do not buy the kind used in potpourri. If you buy it from an herb grower, it's certainly safe to eat.

Prune Armagnac Ice Cream: With added nuggets of brandy-macerated prunes, this ice cream becomes even more exquisite. In a bowl, pour ¼ cup (50 mL) Armagnac, brandy or port over 1 cup (250 mL) chopped prunes. Refrigerate overnight, tossing once or twice to ensure that prunes are coated with Armagnac. Add to ice cream maker in the last 5 minutes of freezing and let machine stir them in.

Honey Vanilla Ice Cream with Strawberry Jam Ripple: A dramatic effect and surprisingly simple to do, rippling or marbling enhances flavor and provides color contrast. There are two methods for creating ribbons of flavor. The second method works well for puréed raspberries and chocolate sauce. For best results, choose marbling colors that are markedly different from that of the ice cream.

1. Remove Honey Vanilla Ice Cream from the machine when it is semisoft and transfer to a freezerproof container. Using a knife or fork, gently swirl 1 tbsp (15 mL) softly set strawberry jam into the ice cream. Cover and freeze until firm.
2. Remove Honey Vanilla Ice Cream from the machine when it is semisoft. Alternately spoon layers of ice cream and softly set jam into a freezerproof container. Make about 3 layers. Using a knife, gently swirl a couple of times. Cover and freeze until firm.

Vanilla Cheesecake Ice Cream

SERVES 8

Marilyn isn't a fan of cheesecake, so the recipe testing for this ice cream fell on Tanya, because her husband, Mike Sheerin, is a sucker for the dessert. So much so that she made a super-sized tub and tasted a spoonful, and he ate the rest. If you are a cheesecake lover, you'll probably do the same.

Tip: Feel free to add bits of different frozen cheesecakes — chocolate or cherry would be a nice addition.

2	eggs	2
1 cup	granulated sugar	250 mL
2 cups	milk	500 mL
1 cup	spreadable cream cheese	250 mL
2 cups	whipping (35%) cream	500 mL
1	small frozen cheesecake, crust included, chopped while frozen into bite-size pieces	1

1. In a bowl, whisk eggs with sugar until thickened and pale yellow. Set aside.

2. In a medium saucepan over medium-low heat, bring milk to a simmer. Gradually whisk into the egg mixture.

3. Return entire mixture to the saucepan. Cook over low heat, stirring constantly, until the mixture is thick enough to coat the back of a wooden spoon. Be careful not to let it boil. Remove from heat and stir in cream cheese until completely melted. Strain into a clean large bowl. Let cool to room temperature.

4. Stir in whipping cream. Cover and refrigerate until completely cold or overnight.

5. Stir cream mixture. Transfer to an ice cream maker and freeze according to manufacturer's instructions. At the semifrozen stage, add cheesecake and continue freezing.

Crème Fraîche Custard Ice Cream

For a sophisticated French twist to regular vanilla ice cream, this recipe uses crème fraîche, a cultured cream similar to but richer than sour cream.

Tip: Double-intensity vanilla packs twice the flavor and aromatic richness of ordinary vanilla, but without extra sugar. It can be purchased at gourmet stores. If you can't find it, use 1 tsp (5 mL) regular vanilla.

4	egg yolks	4
1 cup	whipping (35%) cream	250 mL
⅔ cup	granulated sugar	150 mL
Pinch	sea salt	Pinch
1¼ cups	crème fraîche	300 mL
1 tsp	double-intensity vanilla	5 mL

1. In a bowl, whisk egg yolks until foamy. Set aside.

2. In a medium saucepan, bring cream, sugar and salt to a boil over low heat, stirring to dissolve the sugar. Gradually whisk half the cream mixture into the egg yolks.

3. Gradually whisk the egg mixture back into the saucepan. Cook over low heat, stirring constantly, until the mixture is thick enough to coat the back of a wooden spoon. Be careful not to let it boil. Strain into a clean large bowl. Let cool to room temperature. Cover and refrigerate until completely cold or overnight.

4. Gently stir in crème fraîche and vanilla. Transfer to an ice cream maker and freeze according to manufacturer's instructions.

Crème Brûlée Ice Cream

SERVES 6 TO 8

This ice cream gets its distinctive flavor from the marriage of vanilla and crackled caramelized sugar. The frozen version is just as satisfying, elegant and trendy as the real thing. Although the sugar topping enhances the ice cream, a five-year-old friend informs us that this is not a kid-friendly ice cream, because the shards can be too sharp for little mouths.

Tip: Do not leave the stove when making caramelized sugar because it can easily burn. Caramelized sugar is very hot, so be careful to avoid any contact with hands or mouth until it has cooled completely.

- Candy thermometer
- Baking sheet, greased and lined with foil

Ice Cream

4	egg yolks	4
¾ cup	granulated sugar	175 mL
1	vanilla bean	1
2 cups	milk	500 mL
2 cups	whipping (35%) cream	500 mL

Crackled Caramelized Sugar Topping

¾ cup	granulated sugar	175 mL
2 tbsp	cold water	25 mL
2 tbsp	corn syrup	25 mL

1. *To make Ice Cream:* In a bowl, whisk egg yolks with sugar until thickened and pale yellow. Set aside.

2. Slit vanilla bean lengthwise and scrape seeds into a medium saucepan. Add vanilla pod, milk and cream. Place saucepan over medium-low heat and bring milk mixture just to a simmer. Remove from heat. Let stand for 15 minutes, allowing the flavor of the vanilla to infuse.

3. Discard pod. Bring mixture to a simmer over medium-low heat and simmer for 5 minutes. Gradually whisk into the egg mixture.

4. Return entire mixture to the saucepan. Cook over low heat, stirring constantly, until the mixture is thick enough to coat the back of a wooden spoon. Be careful not to let it boil. Strain into a clean large bowl. Let cool to room temperature. Cover and refrigerate until completely cold or overnight.

5. Stir cream mixture. Transfer to an ice cream maker and freeze according to manufacturer's instructions.

6. *To make Crackled Caramelized Sugar Topping:* In a medium saucepan, stir together sugar, water and corn syrup. Bring to a boil. Cook over medium heat, brushing down the side of the saucepan with cold water occasionally, until candy thermometer registers 300°F (150°C) or mixture turns golden brown.

7. Carefully pour onto prepared baking sheet. Let cool completely. Break into shards. Set aside.

8. When ready to serve, place two scoops of ice cream in a bowl and top with crackled sugar.

❧ Variation

Crème Caramel Ice Cream: To make caramel sauce, increase water in Crackled Caramelized Sugar Topping to ¼ cup (50 mL). Once sugar mixture is golden brown, stir in 1½ cups (375 mL) whipping (35%) cream until foaming subsides. Be very cautious when adding the whipping cream (the mixture will foam and splatter). Hold the saucepan at arm's length and avert your face when adding the cream. To serve, pour caramel sauce over ice cream.

Dulce de Leche Ice Cream

SERVES 4

Dulce de leche, a traditional Latin American topping, has found a place on many desserts, such as this ice cream. It's not just fun to eat but also fun to make because it's so easy — all you have to do is stir the sweetened condensed milk. You won't believe that the caramel is made from that one simple ingredient.

Tips: For soft ice cream, serve immediately. Or freeze overnight until firm.

If cinnamon is not your thing, it's just as delicious without it.

Serving suggestion: Line each cup of a muffin tin with plastic wrap. Pack with ice cream and freeze. Turn the individual portions out onto plates, drizzle with chocolate sauce and sprinkle with unsweetened cocoa powder.

1	can (10 oz/300 mL) sweetened condensed milk	1
1 cup	whipping (35%) cream	250 mL
1 cup	milk	250 mL
1	cinnamon stick (see Tips, left)	1
2 tsp	vanilla	10 mL

1. In a medium saucepan over medium heat, cook condensed milk, stirring constantly, until thick and golden brown, about 15 minutes. Remove from heat.

2. Meanwhile, in a separate medium saucepan over medium-low heat, bring cream, milk and cinnamon stick to a simmer. Remove cinnamon stick.

3. Very slowly and carefully to prevent spattering, pour condensed milk into a clean large bowl. Gradually whisk in cream mixture, holding the saucepan at arm's length and averting your face when adding the cream. Whisk in vanilla. Cover and refrigerate until completely cold or overnight.

4. Stir cream mixture. Transfer to an ice cream maker and freeze according to manufacturer's instructions.

❧ Variation

Traditional Dulce de Leche: If you're not in an ice cream mood, do as they do in Latin American countries: cook the sweetened condensed milk down into dulce de leche and, instead of freezing it into ice cream, spread it on toast or your favorite pound cake.

Classic Chocolate Ice Cream (page 22)

Neapolitan Ice Cream Sundaes (page 23)

Dulce de Leche Ice Cream (page 48)

Dulce de Leche and Fleur de Sel Ice Cream

Fleur de sel is a French sea salt that is all the rage right now. More of a finishing salt than a cooking salt, its tiny diamond-like crystals add a gourmet kick to caramel ice cream.

Tip: Be careful not to pour the hot milk into the egg mixture too quickly. You don't want to scramble the eggs.

1	can (10 oz/300 mL) condensed milk	1
3	egg yolks	3
½ cup	granulated sugar	125 mL
2 cups	milk	500 mL
2 cups	whipping (35%) cream	500 mL
1 tsp	fleur de sel, divided	5 mL

1. In a medium saucepan over medium heat, cook condensed milk, stirring constantly, until thick and golden brown, about 15 minutes. Remove dulce de leche from heat and set aside.

2. In a bowl, whisk egg yolks with sugar until thickened and pale yellow. Set aside.

3. In another medium saucepan over medium-low heat, bring milk to a simmer. Gradually whisk into the egg mixture.

4. Return entire mixture to the saucepan. Add dulce de leche and cook over low heat, stirring constantly, until the mixture is thick enough to coat the back of a wooden spoon. Be careful not to let it boil. Strain into a clean large bowl. Let cool to room temperature.

5. Stir in whipping cream and half the fleur de sel. Cover and refrigerate until completely cold or overnight.

6. Stir cream mixture. Transfer to an ice cream maker and freeze according to manufacturer's instructions.

7. Serve sprinkled with the remaining fleur de sel (only a few flakes are necessary).

Tiramisu Ice Cream

This traditional Italian layered dessert is now on many ice cream shop menus. Because it is meant to be shown off as well as enjoyed, we layer ours in a pretty glass bowl and return it to the freezer until firm. You can also spoon it into parfait glasses and freeze until you're ready to serve.

1 cup	granulated sugar, divided	250 mL
1 cup	water	250 mL
1 cup	mascarpone cheese	250 mL
1 cup	cream cheese, softened	250 mL
1½ tsp	vanilla	7 mL
3 tbsp	boiling water	45 mL
1 tbsp	instant coffee granules	15 mL
3 tbsp	coffee-flavored liqueur	45 mL
3 oz	ladyfingers (about 6)	90 g
¼ cup	unsweetened cocoa powder	50 mL
¼ cup	bittersweet chocolate shavings	50 mL

1. Combine ¾ cup (175 mL) sugar and 1 cup (250 mL) water in a medium saucepan. Cook over medium-low heat, stirring, until sugar is dissolved. Let cool to room temperature, about 15 minutes.

2. In a medium bowl, beat mascarpone cheese with a wooden spoon until soft. Stir in cream cheese. Whisk in sugar syrup, 2 tbsp (25 mL) at a time, until well blended. Stir in vanilla. Cover and refrigerate until completely cold or overnight.

3. Meanwhile, in a bowl, stir together boiling water, remaining sugar and instant coffee. Stir in liqueur. Let cool to room temperature, about 15 minutes.

4. Stir cheese mixture. Transfer to an ice cream maker and freeze according to manufacturer's instructions.

5. Crumble ladyfingers into small pieces. Toss with coffee mixture. Set aside.

6. Spoon one-third of the ice cream into a freezerproof container, glass serving bowl or parfait glasses. Layer half of the biscuit mixture over top. Repeat layers once. Top with remaining ice cream. Freeze for 2 to 3 hours or until firm.

7. To serve, dust with cocoa and sprinkle with chocolate shavings.

Christmas Pudding Ice Cream

SERVES 8 TO 10

You might not think of making ice cream in the wintertime, but this recipe works perfectly at the end of a holiday meal and is a great way to use up extra Christmas pudding or Christmas cake.

2	egg yolks	2
1 cup	granulated sugar	250 mL
2 cups	milk	500 mL
2 cups	whipping (35%) cream	500 mL
1 cup	crumbled Christmas pudding or cake	250 mL
1 tbsp	vanilla	15 mL
1 tsp	ground cinnamon	5 mL
1 tsp	ground nutmeg	5 mL

1. In a bowl, whisk egg yolks with sugar until thickened and pale yellow. Set aside.

2. In a medium saucepan over medium-low heat, bring milk to a simmer. Gradually whisk into the egg mixture.

3. Return entire mixture to the saucepan. Cook over low heat, stirring constantly, until the mixture is thick enough to coat the back of a wooden spoon. Be careful not to let it boil. Strain into a clean large bowl. Let cool to room temperature.

4. Stir in whipping cream, Christmas pudding, vanilla, cinnamon and nutmeg. Cover and refrigerate until completely cold or overnight.

5. Stir cream mixture. Transfer to an ice cream maker and freeze according to manufacturer's instructions.

Brown Sugar Ice Cream

4	egg yolks	4
¾ cup	packed brown sugar	175 mL
1½ cups	table (18%) cream	375 mL
½ cup	2% milk (see Tip, page 106)	125 mL
1 cup	whipping (35%) cream	250 mL
2 tsp	vanilla	10 mL
Pinch	salt	Pinch

1. In a bowl, whisk egg yolks with brown sugar until thickened and pale yellow. Set aside.

2. In a medium saucepan over medium-low heat, bring table cream and milk to a simmer. Gradually whisk into the egg mixture.

3. Return entire mixture to the saucepan. Cook over low heat, stirring constantly, until the mixture is thick enough to coat the back of a wooden spoon. Be careful not to let it boil. Strain into a clean large bowl. Let cool to room temperature.

4. Stir in whipping cream, vanilla and salt. Cover and refrigerate until completely cold or overnight.

5. Stir cream mixture. Transfer to an ice cream maker and freeze according to manufacturer's instructions.

Caramel Ice Cream

SERVES 4 TO 6

This good old-fashioned custard cream is very rich, but it's also very rewarding with its wonderful taste. We love this ice cream with bananas sautéed with brown sugar, butter and a dash of rum.

Tip: To make vanilla sugar, place vanilla pod in an airtight container with granulated sugar. Store for 1 week to let flavor infuse. Use to flavor whipped cream, custards or dessert sauces.

Serving suggestion: Line a 9- by 5-inch (2 L) loaf pan with plastic wrap. Spread 4 cups (1 L) softened Caramel Ice Cream in pan. Smooth top with a spatula. Freeze for 1 hour or until firm. Cover ice cream with 4 cups (1 L) softened chocolate ice cream. Smooth top. Freeze for 1 hour or until firm. To serve, unwrap and turn out of pan onto a cutting board. Using a knife dipped in hot water, cut into slices.

1	vanilla bean	1
6	egg yolks	6
1 cup	granulated sugar	250 mL
¼ cup	water	50 mL
1 cup	whipping (35%) cream	250 mL
1 cup	milk	250 mL

1. Slit vanilla bean lengthwise. Scrape seeds into a bowl. Discard pod or make vanilla sugar for later use (see Tip, left). Whisk in egg yolks until pale yellow. Set aside.

2. In a medium saucepan over medium-low heat, stir sugar with water until sugar is dissolved. Cook, stirring constantly, until deep amber color.

3. Remove from heat. (Be careful to avert your face and hold the saucepan away from you because cold cream meeting hot caramel means dangerous spatters.) Add cream and milk, stirring until foaming subsides. Return to heat. Cook, stirring constantly, for 5 minutes or until a velvety caramel sauce forms. Gradually whisk into the egg mixture.

4. Transfer entire mixture to a clean saucepan. Cook over low heat, stirring constantly, until the mixture is thick enough to coat the back of a wooden spoon. Be careful not to let it boil. Strain into a clean large bowl. Let cool to room temperature. Cover and refrigerate until completely cold or overnight.

5. Stir cream mixture. Transfer to an ice cream maker and freeze according to manufacturer's instructions.

Black Pepper and Cloves Ice Cream

Ground black pepper pairs beautifully with the cloves in this unusual ice cream, which is preferred by adults. Serve it with fresh strawberries or alongside a bowl full of fresh sweet cherries in summer; try it alongside warm plum pudding or fruitcake at Christmas.

2	egg yolks	2
1 cup	granulated sugar	250 mL
1½ cups	milk	375 mL
1½ cups	whipping (35%) cream	375 mL
1 tbsp	freshly ground black pepper	15 mL
1 tbsp	ground cloves	15 mL

1. In a bowl, whisk egg yolks with sugar until thickened and pale yellow. Set aside.

2. In a medium saucepan over medium-low heat, bring milk and cream to a simmer. Gradually whisk 1 cup (250 mL) of the hot milk mixture into the egg mixture.

3. Gradually whisk egg mixture back into the saucepan. Cook over low heat, stirring constantly, until the mixture is thick enough to coat the back of a wooden spoon. Be careful not to let it boil. Strain into a clean large bowl. Let cool to room temperature.

4. Stir in black pepper and cloves. Cover and refrigerate until completely cold or overnight.

5. Stir cream mixture. Transfer to an ice cream maker and freeze according to manufacturer's instructions.

Cinnamon Stick Ice Cream

SERVES 4 TO 6

Cinnamon is a key ingredient in many desserts, but this time we made it the star. Our secret is to double the cinnamon by steeping a cinnamon stick in the cream in addition to adding some of the ground variety to the custard before freezing.

3 cups	table (18%) cream	750 mL
¾ cup	granulated sugar	175 mL
1	cinnamon stick	1
1 tbsp	ground cinnamon	15 mL
1 tsp	vanilla	5 mL

1. In a medium saucepan over medium-low heat, bring cream, sugar and cinnamon stick to a simmer.

2. Strain into a clean large bowl. Whisk in ground cinnamon and vanilla. Let stand for 30 minutes.

3. Cover and refrigerate until completely cold or overnight. Remove cinnamon stick.

4. Stir cream mixture. Transfer to an ice cream maker and freeze according to manufacturer's instructions.

❧ Variations

Red-Hot Cinnamon Ice Cream: For a Valentine's Day treat, add ¼ cup (50 mL) red-hot heart candies in the last 5 minutes of freezing. Or sprinkle candies over each serving of Cinnamon Stick Ice Cream.

Cinnamon Nutmeg Ice Cream: Add 2 tsp (10 mL) ground nutmeg along with the ground cinnamon.

Crunchy Cinnamon Toast Ice Cream

SERVES 8 TO 10

You might not think it's cool to eat ice cream for breakfast, but this dessert does have a comforting morning quality about it.

4	egg yolks	4
1 cup	granulated sugar	250 mL
2 cups	milk	500 mL
1 tbsp	ground cinnamon	15 mL
2 cups	whipping (35%) cream	500 mL
1 tsp	vanilla	5 mL

Cinnamon Toast

4	slices whole wheat bread	4
2 tbsp	butter	25 mL
1 tbsp	ground cinnamon	15 mL
1 tbsp	granulated sugar	15 mL

1. In a bowl, whisk egg yolks with sugar until thickened and pale yellow. Set aside.

2. In a medium saucepan over medium-low heat, bring milk and cinnamon to a simmer. Gradually whisk into the egg mixture.

3. Return entire mixture to the saucepan. Cook over low heat, stirring constantly, until the mixture is thick enough to coat the back of a wooden spoon. Be careful not to let it boil. Strain into a clean large bowl. Let cool to room temperature.

4. Stir in whipping cream and vanilla. Cover and refrigerate until completely cold or overnight.

5. *To make Cinnamon Toast:* Lightly toast bread. In a medium saucepan, melt butter over medium heat. Stir in cinnamon and sugar; heat until butter is bubbly. Add the lightly toasted bread in batches and fry, turning once, until crisp and golden on both sides. Transfer to paper towels and let cool. Chop into bite-size pieces.

6. Stir cream mixture. Transfer to an ice cream maker and freeze according to manufacturer's instructions. Add chopped cinnamon toast in the last 5 minutes of freezing and let machine stir it in.

Ginger Ice Cream

SERVES 6

Ginger is a fiery, feisty spice that adds a refreshing kick to this vanilla-based ice cream. It's great plain, drizzled with chocolate sauce or topped with fruit salad.

Tip: Crystallized or candied ginger has already been cooked in a sugar syrup and coated with coarse sugar. If you want to add more sweet heat to the ice cream, you can increase the amount to 1 cup (250 mL).

Serving suggestion: In a food processor or blender, purée 1 mango, pitted and peeled, with ¼ cup (50 mL) of additional crystallized ginger. Spoon over Ginger Ice Cream or vanilla ice cream and serve.

4	egg yolks	4
¾ cup	granulated sugar	175 mL
2 cups	whipping (35%) cream	500 mL
2 cups	milk	500 mL
¾ cup	crystallized ginger, finely chopped (see Tip, left)	175 mL
¼ tsp	vanilla	1 mL

1. In a bowl, whisk egg yolks with sugar until thickened and pale yellow. Set aside.

2. In a medium saucepan over medium-low heat, bring cream, milk and ginger to a simmer. Gradually whisk into the egg mixture.

3. Return entire mixture to the saucepan. Cook over low heat, stirring constantly, until the mixture is thick enough to coat the back of a wooden spoon. Be careful not to let it boil. Strain into a clean large bowl. Let cool to room temperature.

4. Stir in vanilla. Cover and refrigerate until completely cold or overnight.

5. Stir cream mixture. Transfer to an ice cream maker and freeze according to manufacturer's instructions.

Variation

Chocolate Ginger Ice Cream: Add 12 oz (375 g) bittersweet chocolate to hot cream mixture and proceed with the recipe.

Ginger Molasses Ice Cream

Molasses, once a household staple, will become a favorite ingredient once you try this special recipe. For a festive ice cream sandwich, squish a scoop of this ice cream between two gingersnap cookies.

3	eggs	3
½ cup	granulated sugar	125 mL
1½ cups	whipping (35%) cream	375 mL
1 cup	milk	250 mL
⅓ cup	fancy molasses	75 mL
¼ cup	finely chopped crystallized ginger	50 mL
½ tsp	vanilla	2 mL

1. In a bowl, whisk eggs with sugar until thickened and pale yellow. Set aside.

2. In a medium saucepan over medium-low heat, bring cream and milk to a simmer. Gradually whisk into the egg mixture.

3. Return entire mixture to the saucepan. Cook over low heat, stirring constantly, until the mixture is thick enough to coat the back of a wooden spoon. Be careful not to let it boil. Strain into a clean large bowl. Let cool to room temperature.

4. Stir in molasses, ginger and vanilla. Cover and refrigerate until completely cold or overnight.

5. Stir cream mixture. Transfer to an ice cream maker and freeze according to manufacturer's instructions.

Ginger Cinnamon Ice Cream

The addition of cinnamon makes this ginger pleaser deliciously complex.

2	egg yolks	2
1 cup	granulated sugar	250 mL
1½ cups	milk	375 mL
1½ cups	whipping (35%) cream	375 mL
1 tbsp	grated gingerroot	15 mL
1 tbsp	ground cinnamon	15 mL
1 tsp	ground ginger	5 mL

1. In a bowl, whisk egg yolks with sugar until thickened and pale yellow. Set aside.

2. In a medium saucepan over medium-low heat, bring milk and cream to a simmer. Gradually whisk 1 cup (250 mL) of the hot milk mixture into the egg mixture.

3. Gradually whisk egg mixture back into the saucepan. Cook over low heat, stirring constantly, until the mixture is thick enough to coat the back of a wooden spoon. Be careful not to let it boil. Strain into a clean large bowl. Let cool to room temperature.

4. Stir in grated ginger, cinnamon and ground ginger. Cover and refrigerate until completely cold or overnight.

5. Stir cream mixture. Transfer to an ice cream maker and freeze according to manufacturer's instructions.

Honey, Lemon and Thyme Ice Cream

Steeping the thyme in the cream mixture brings out the subtle taste of this favorite summer herb.

Tip: Experiment with different kinds of thyme — each variety brings its own flavor.

2 cups	whipping (35%) cream	500 mL
1 cup	milk	250 mL
¾ cup	fresh thyme sprigs	175 mL
	Grated zest of 1 lemon	
2	eggs	2
¼ cup	granulated sugar	50 mL
½ cup	liquid honey	125 mL

1. In a medium saucepan, bring cream, milk, thyme and lemon zest to a boil. Remove from heat, cover and let steep at room temperature for 1½ hours. Remove thyme sprigs. Reheat over medium heat until steaming.

2. In a bowl, whisk eggs with sugar until thickened and pale yellow. Stir in honey. Gradually whisk in cream mixture.

3. Return entire mixture to the saucepan. Cook over low heat, stirring constantly, until the mixture is thick enough to coat the back of a wooden spoon. Be careful not to let it boil. Strain into a clean large bowl. Let cool to room temperature. Cover and refrigerate until completely cold or overnight.

4. Stir cream mixture. Transfer to an ice cream maker and freeze according to manufacturer's instructions. When serving, garnish ice cream with fresh thyme leaves.

Mint Ice Cream

SERVES 6

When your patch of mint has taken over, this is a great way to use some of it up. A drizzle of melted dark chocolate takes this dessert to the next level.

2	egg yolks	2
⅔ cup	granulated sugar	150 mL
1½ cups	whipping (35%) cream	375 mL
⅔ cup	milk	150 mL
1½ cups	packed fresh mint leaves	375 mL

1. In a bowl, whisk egg yolks with sugar until thickened and pale yellow. Set aside.

2. In a food processor or blender, purée cream, milk and mint leaves until smooth.

3. Transfer cream mixture to a medium saucepan and bring to a simmer over medium-low heat. Gradually whisk into the egg mixture.

4. Return entire mixture to the saucepan. Cook over low heat, stirring constantly, until the mixture is thick enough to coat the back of a wooden spoon. Be careful not to let it boil. Strain into a clean large bowl. Let cool to room temperature. Cover and refrigerate until completely cold or overnight.

5. Stir cream mixture. Transfer to an ice cream maker and freeze according to manufacturer's instructions.

Variation

Chunk this ice cream up with your favorite chocolate brownies, broken up and mixed in when the ice cream is at its soft stage.

Rosemary Ice Cream

SERVES 6 TO 8

Want an elegant ice cream to serve at your next dinner party? Try this simple yet sophisticated recipe for rosemary-infused ice cream. Its sweet, aromatic flavor is sure to be a delicious topic of conversation at any table.

Tip: For more intense flavor, simmer the rosemary-cream mixture for 30 minutes. For just a hint of rosemary flavor, simmer the mixture for 5 minutes.

Serving suggestions: Line a muffin tin with paper muffin cups. Place one scoop of Rosemary Ice Cream into each cup. Freeze until firm. When ready to serve, lift out the cups and tear off the paper liners for tidy, one-serving portions. Or place two scoops in a bowl and garnish with a small sprig of fresh rosemary and a sugar, shortbread or lavender cookie.

3	egg yolks	3
½ cup	granulated sugar	125 mL
1 tbsp	packed brown sugar	15 mL
2 cups	table (18%) cream	500 mL
2 cups	milk	500 mL
4	sprigs fresh rosemary (see Tips, left and page 184)	4

1. In a bowl, whisk egg yolks with granulated and brown sugars until thickened and pale yellow. Set aside.

2. In a medium saucepan over medium-low heat, bring cream, milk and rosemary to a simmer. Simmer, stirring occasionally, for 15 minutes. Discard rosemary. Gradually whisk hot cream mixture into the egg mixture.

3. Return entire mixture to the saucepan. Cook over low heat, stirring constantly, until the mixture is thick enough to coat the back of a wooden spoon. Be careful not to let it boil. Strain into a clean large bowl. Let cool to room temperature. Cover and refrigerate until completely cold or overnight.

4. Stir cream mixture. Transfer to an ice cream maker and freeze according to manufacturer's instructions.

❧ Variation
Lavender Ice Cream: Substitute 4 sprigs fresh lavender flowers for the rosemary.

Fruity
Ice Creams

continued on next page...

Cranberry Ice Cream

SERVES 8

This ice cream is the perfect side to Christmas cake. Feel free to add some chopped chocolate with the dried cranberries, if you wish.

3	egg yolks	3
1 cup	granulated sugar	250 mL
2 cups	milk	500 mL
2 cups	whipping (35%) cream	500 mL
2 cups	unsweetened cranberry juice	500 mL
1 tsp	vanilla	5 mL
½ cup	finely chopped dried cranberries	125 mL

1. In a bowl, whisk egg yolks with sugar until thickened and pale yellow. Set aside.

2. In a medium saucepan over medium-low heat, bring milk to a simmer. Gradually whisk into the egg mixture.

3. Return entire mixture to the saucepan. Cook over low heat, stirring constantly, until the mixture is thick enough to coat the back of a wooden spoon. Be careful not to let it boil. Strain into a clean large bowl. Let cool to room temperature.

4. Stir in whipping cream, cranberry juice and vanilla. Cover and refrigerate until completely cold or overnight.

5. Stir cream mixture. Transfer to an ice cream maker and freeze according to manufacturer's instructions. Add cranberries in the last 5 minutes of freezing and let machine stir them in.

Raspberry-Blackberry Ice Cream

Refreshing and satisfying, this ice cream makes the perfect summer treat.

2 cups	raspberries	500 mL
2 cups	blackberries	500 mL
2	eggs	2
1 cup	granulated sugar	250 mL
1 cup	milk	250 mL
1 cup	whipping (35%) cream	250 mL
1 tsp	vanilla	5 mL

1. In a food processor or blender, purée raspberries and blackberries until smooth. Using the back of a wooden spoon, press through a fine sieve into a bowl to remove seeds. Set aside.

2. In a bowl, whisk eggs with sugar until thickened and pale yellow. Set aside.

3. In a medium saucepan over medium-low heat, bring milk to a simmer. Gradually whisk into the egg mixture.

4. Return entire mixture to the saucepan. Cook over low heat, stirring constantly, until the mixture is thick enough to coat the back of a wooden spoon. Be careful not to let it boil. Strain into a clean large bowl. Let cool to room temperature.

5. Stir in whipping cream, vanilla and puréed fruit. Cover and refrigerate until completely cold or overnight.

6. Stir cream mixture. Transfer to an ice cream maker and freeze according to manufacturer's instructions.

Variation

Feel free to switch up the berries — any combination will work well.

Strawberries and Cream
Ice Cream

This intensely fruity ice cream is best made with the sweetest and juiciest of fresh berries. It's terrific on its own or as a topping for waffles and crêpes.

Tip: If possible, taste the berries before buying them to ensure the best flavor.

Serving suggestion: For a quick Strawberry Sauce, in a food processor or blender, purée 1 cup (250 mL) additional strawberries with 2 tbsp (25 mL) orange juice, Cointreau or white vermouth. Pour over ice cream.

2 cups	whipping (35%) cream	500 mL
½ cup	granulated sugar	125 mL
4 cups	fresh strawberries, hulled	1 L
¼ cup	freshly squeezed orange juice	50 mL
1 tbsp	orange zest	15 mL

1. In a medium saucepan over medium-low heat, bring cream to a simmer. Stir in sugar. Cook, stirring, until sugar is dissolved. Let cool to room temperature.

2. In a food processor or blender, purée strawberries with orange juice until smooth. Stir into cream mixture along with orange zest. Cover and refrigerate until completely cold or overnight.

3. Transfer to an ice cream maker and freeze according to manufacturer's instructions.

Super-Easy Strawberry and Lime Ice Cream

SERVES 6

Want a super-quick, super-delicious ice cream? Well, we have one for you. There's no custard, no chilling overnight and no churning in the machine. Just mix the ingredients and freeze. Don't believe us? Go ahead, give it a try.

2 cups	strawberries	500 mL
	Juice of 2 limes	
1 cup	confectioner's (icing) sugar	250 mL
2 cups	whipping (35%) cream	500 mL

1. In a food processor or blender, purée strawberries and lime juice until smooth. Using the back of a wooden spoon, press through a fine sieve into a bowl to remove seeds.

2. Whisk in confectioner's sugar until dissolved. Whisk in whipping cream until soft peaks form (you can use a handheld electric mixer if it's easier).

3. Spoon into an airtight container and smooth top. Freeze for at least 6 hours or overnight.

Strawberry-Rhubarb Ice Cream

The combination of these two fruits is a classic, so much so that it's worth the extra effort to prepare and cook the rhubarb.

Tip: You can use either fresh or frozen rhubarb.

2 cups	chopped rhubarb, about ½-inch (1 cm) pieces	500 mL
½ cup	water	125 mL
2	eggs	2
⅔ cup	granulated sugar	150 mL
1 cup	milk	250 mL
1 cup	whipping (35%) cream	250 mL
2 cups	chopped ripe strawberries	500 mL

1. In a medium saucepan over medium heat, bring rhubarb and water to a simmer. Cook, stirring occasionally, for 15 minutes or until rhubarb is soft and mixture resembles thick applesauce. Using the back of a wooden spoon, push through a fine sieve. Set aside.

2. In a bowl, whisk eggs with sugar until thickened and pale yellow. Set aside.

3. In a separate medium saucepan over medium-low heat, bring milk and cream to a simmer. Gradually whisk into the egg mixture.

4. Return entire mixture to the saucepan. Cook over low heat, stirring constantly, until the mixture is thick enough to coat the back of a wooden spoon. Be careful not to let it boil. Strain into a clean large bowl. Let cool to room temperature.

5. Stir in rhubarb mixture and strawberries. Cover and refrigerate until completely cold or overnight.

6. Stir cream mixture. Transfer to an ice cream maker and freeze according to manufacturer's instructions.

❧ Variation
Ginger Strawberry-Rhubarb Ice Cream: Add 2 tbsp (25 mL) chopped crystallized ginger to the strained cream mixture.

Cherries and Cream Ice Cream

SERVES 4

If you prefer non-custardy ice cream, this is a wonderful and simple recipe that also works well with summer's fresh dark, sweet, juicy fruit.

Tip: If you're using fresh cherries, make sure they're plump and ripe. The best way to remove their pits is to invest in a cherry pitter. These inexpensive timesaving gadgets can be found at many hardware stores and most kitchen stores.

1 cup	whipping (35%) cream	250 mL
½ cup	milk	125 mL
½ cup	granulated sugar	125 mL
1 cup	pitted fresh sweet cherries (see Tip, left) or 1 can (14 oz/398 mL) pitted sweet cherries, drained	250 mL

1. In a medium saucepan over medium-low heat, bring cream and milk to a simmer. Add sugar and cook, stirring, until sugar is dissolved. Be careful not to let it boil. Strain into a clean large bowl. Let cool to room temperature.

2. In a food processor or blender, purée cherries until smooth. Stir into cream mixture. Cover and refrigerate until completely cold or overnight.

3. Stir cream mixture. Transfer to an ice cream maker and freeze according to manufacturer's instructions.

Cherry Custard Ice Cream

SERVES 6

Enjoy the summery taste of cherries year-round with this luscious recipe. You could use fresh cherries, but why not save them for eating and use frozen or canned cherries here instead?

2	egg yolks	2
¾ cup	granulated sugar	175 mL
1 cup	milk	250 mL
1	can (14 oz/398 mL) pitted sweet cherries in syrup	1
1½ cups	whipping (35%) cream	375 mL

1. In a bowl, whisk egg yolks with sugar until thickened and pale yellow. Set aside.

2. In a medium saucepan over medium-low heat, bring milk to a simmer. Gradually whisk into the egg mixture.

3. Return entire mixture to the saucepan. Cook over low heat, stirring constantly, until the mixture is thick enough to coat the back of a wooden spoon. Be careful not to let it boil. Strain into a clean large bowl. Let cool to room temperature.

4. In a food processor or blender, purée cherries with syrup until almost smooth. Stir cherry mixture along with cream into milk mixture. Cover and refrigerate until completely cold or overnight.

5. Stir cream mixture. Transfer to an ice cream maker and freeze according to manufacturer's instructions.

❧ Variation

Cherry Custard Chocolate Marble Ice Cream: When the ice cream is semifrozen, stop the ice cream maker and scoop ice cream into a freezerproof container. Using a knife, swirl in ¼ cup (50 mL) melted dark chocolate to create marbled effect. Freeze until firm.

Caramelized Pear and Spiced Pecan Ice Cream

SERVES 8

This ice cream requires a bit of make-ahead work, but the results are worth it. We had the best results when we put the caramelized pear chunks and spiced pecans in the freezer before adding them to the ice cream.

- 2 baking sheets, lined with parchment paper

Caramelized Pears

1/4 cup	butter	50 mL
1/2 cup	granulated sugar	125 mL
2	firm pears, peeled and chopped into 1/2-inch (1 cm) chunks	2

Ice Cream

2	eggs	2
1/2 cup	granulated sugar	125 mL
1 1/2 cups	whipping (35%) cream	375 mL
1 1/2 cups	milk	375 mL
1 tbsp	vanilla	15 mL
1 tsp	ground cinnamon	5 mL

Spiced Pecans

1	egg white	1
1 tbsp	water	15 mL
1/4 tsp	vanilla	1 mL
2 cups	pecans, coarsely chopped	500 mL
1/4 cup	granulated sugar	50 mL
1/2 tsp	ground cinnamon	2 mL
1/4 tsp	salt	1 mL
1/4 tsp	ground cloves	1 mL
1/4 tsp	ground ginger	1 mL

1. *To make Caramelized Pears:* In a skillet, melt butter over medium heat. Add sugar and cook, stirring, until the mixture starts to turn golden. Add pears, stir to coat and cook for 20 to 30 minutes, or until golden brown on all sides. Pour onto one of the prepared baking sheets and separate the pieces so they don't stick together. Let cool slightly. Freeze for at least 2 hours or overnight.

2. *To make Ice Cream:* In a bowl, whisk eggs with sugar until thickened and pale yellow. Set aside.

3. In a medium saucepan over medium-low heat, bring cream and milk to a simmer. Gradually whisk into the egg mixture.

4. Return entire mixture to saucepan. Cook over low heat, stirring constantly, until the mixture is thick enough to coat the back of a wooden spoon. Be careful not to let it boil. Strain into a clean large bowl. Let cool to room temperature.

5. Stir in vanilla and cinnamon. Cover and refrigerate until completely cold or overnight.

6. *To make Spiced Pecans:* Preheat oven to 350°F (180°C). In a bowl, whisk together egg white, water and vanilla. Add pecans and toss to coat completely. In a large plastic bag, combine sugar, cinnamon, salt, cloves and ginger. Add pecans, shaking bag to coat completely. Spread on a prepared baking sheet and bake for 30 minutes, stirring once. Let cool slightly. Freeze for 2 hours.

7. Stir cream mixture. Transfer to an ice cream maker and freeze according to manufacturer's instructions. Add pears and pecans in the last 5 minutes of freezing and let machine stir them in.

Apple Brown Betty Ice Cream

SERVES 6 TO 8

Apple butter isn't just for toast, as we discovered in this ice cream that offers a definite taste of autumn in Canada. We also like it served on crêpes for brunch. Rich and spicy gingersnaps give it texture and color.

Tip: To cook custard: Cook over low heat, stirring constantly, for about 15 minutes. When custard thickens and coats the back of a wooden spoon without dripping, it's ready. A good way to test thickness is to drag your finger along the back of the coated spoon to see if a line appears.

Serving suggestions: Serve in hollowed-out apples and dust with cinnamon sugar.

For a Halloween treat, drizzle top with melted chocolate in a spiderweb pattern.

1 cup	granulated sugar	250 mL
2	eggs	2
1	egg yolk	1
2 tsp	all-purpose flour	10 mL
1 cup	table (18%) cream	250 mL
1 1/2 cups	apple butter	375 mL
1/2 tsp	ground cinnamon	2 mL
1 tsp	vanilla	5 mL
1 cup	whipping (35%) cream	250 mL
1 cup	crumbled gingersnaps	250 mL

1. In a bowl, whisk together sugar, eggs and egg yolk until thickened and pale yellow. Whisk in flour. Set aside.

2. In a medium saucepan over medium-low heat, bring table cream to a simmer. Gradually whisk into egg mixture. Return entire mixture to the saucepan. Cook over low heat, stirring constantly, until the mixture is thick enough to coat the back of a wooden spoon (see Tip, left). Be careful not to let it boil or the eggs will scramble.

3. Remove from heat and whisk in apple butter and cinnamon. Strain into a clean large bowl. Add vanilla. Cover and refrigerate until completely cold or overnight.

4. Stir in whipping cream. Transfer to an ice cream maker and freeze according to manufacturer's instructions. In the last 5 minutes of freezing, add crumbled gingersnaps and let machine stir them in.

5. Ice cream will be soft. For firmer ice cream, place in the freezer for at least 2 hours.

Variation

Instead of the gingersnaps, 1 cup (250 mL) cinnamon granola would also be yummy and would add a nice texture to the ice cream.

Orange Marmalade Ice Cream

This ice cream is so easy to make that it's almost like cheating. It uses store-bought marmalade, requires no cooking and is soft, luscious and oh-so-delicious.

Tip: This ice cream can be a little softer than egg-based ice creams, so don't worry if it's a little sloppy. If you prefer it harder, pop it in the freezer overnight.

2 cups	orange marmalade	500 mL
1 tbsp	vanilla	15 mL
1 tbsp	orange extract	15 mL
2 cups	table (18%) cream	500 mL
2 cups	milk	500 mL

1. In a large bowl, stir together marmalade, vanilla and orange extract. Stir in cream and milk.

2. Cover and refrigerate until completely cold or overnight.

3. Transfer to an ice cream maker and freeze according to manufacturer's instructions.

Variation

Jam Ice Cream: Omit orange extract. Instead of the orange marmalade, substitute your favorite jam, such as raspberry, apricot or strawberry.

Orange Custard Ice Cream

This tangy and creamy ice cream gets its flavor from the combination of whipping cream and buttermilk. One spoonful and you'll be transported back in time to the hot, hazy summer days of your childhood. Serve it plain or garnished with a sprig of fresh mint or a piece of orange-flavored chocolate.

Tip: If you adore orange, you can increase the amount of orange extract to 3 tbsp (45 mL).

Serving suggestion: For a fancy dinner party, slice one-third off the tops of 6 oranges. (You will need an additional orange for zesting.) Set tops aside. Squeeze juice out of bottoms, then scrape out any membranes. Scoop Orange Custard Ice Cream into shells. Top with lids. Freeze until firm.

5	egg yolks	5
1¼ cups	granulated sugar	300 mL
2 cups	whipping (35%) cream	500 mL
2 cups	buttermilk	500 mL
	Zest of 1 orange	
½ cup	freshly squeezed orange juice	125 mL
2 tbsp	orange extract	25 mL

1. In a bowl, whisk egg yolks with sugar until thickened and pale yellow. Set aside.

2. In a medium saucepan over medium-low heat, bring cream and buttermilk to a simmer. Gradually whisk into the egg mixture.

3. Return entire mixture to the saucepan. Cook over low heat, stirring constantly, until the mixture is thick enough to coat the back of a wooden spoon. Be careful not to let it boil. Strain into a clean large bowl. Let cool to room temperature.

4. Stir in orange zest, orange juice and orange extract. Cover and refrigerate until completely cold or overnight.

5. Stir cream mixture. Transfer to an ice cream maker and freeze according to manufacturer's instructions.

Variations

Chocolate Orange Custard Ice Cream: Add ½ cup (125 mL) shaved orange-flavored chocolate in the last 5 minutes of freezing and let machine stir it in.

Orange Lime Custard Ice Cream: Reduce orange juice to ¼ cup (50 mL) and add ¼ cup (50 mL) freshly squeezed lime juice.

Orange Shredded Wheat Crisps

*For a crunchy topping to almost any ice cream or frozen yogurt,
make these orange crisps one day ahead and store them
in an airtight container.*

- Preheat oven to 350°F (180°C)
- Rimmed baking sheet, greased

2	large shredded wheat cereal biscuits	2
1 tbsp	unsalted butter, melted	15 mL
2 tsp	packed brown sugar	10 mL
1/2 tsp	orange zest	2 mL

1. Crumble biscuits into a bowl. Toss with butter, brown sugar and orange zest. Place on prepared baking sheet.

2. Bake in preheated oven until golden, about 10 minutes. Let cool to room temperature.

3. Serve as a topping for ice cream or frozen yogurt or mix into your favorite in the last 5 minutes of freezing and let machine stir it in.

❧ SERVES 6

Grapefruit Lime
Ice Cream

SERVES 8

Get ready to pucker up! Grapefruit and limes make such a sour and refreshing combination, we couldn't resist turning it into an ice cream.

2	eggs	2
1 cup	granulated sugar	250 mL
2 cups	milk	500 mL
2 cups	whipping (35%) cream	500 mL
	Grated zest and juice of 3 limes	
	Grated zest and juice of 2 grapefruit	

1. In a bowl, whisk eggs with sugar until thickened and pale yellow. Set aside.

2. In a medium saucepan over medium-low heat, bring milk to a simmer. Gradually whisk into the egg mixture.

3. Return entire mixture to the saucepan. Cook over low heat, stirring constantly, until the mixture is thick enough to coat the back of a wooden spoon. Be careful not to let it boil. Strain into a clean large bowl. Let cool to room temperature.

4. Stir in whipping cream, lime zest, lime juice, grapefruit zest and grapefruit juice. Cover and refrigerate until completely cold or overnight.

5. Stir cream mixture. Transfer to an ice cream maker and freeze according to manufacturer's instructions.

Key Lime Ice Cream

A popular, and less fussy, method of making ice cream is to use condensed milk as the base. In this version, the fat of traditional ice cream is substantially reduced (thanks to the partly skimmed condensed milk) without sacrificing taste. Use bottled key lime juice (now available at many gourmet grocery stores) rather than juice from traditional limes.

1	can (10 oz/300 mL) sweetened condensed partly skimmed milk	1
1 cup	Simple Syrup (see recipe, page 20)	250 mL
½ cup	key lime juice	125 mL

1. In a bowl, stir together condensed milk, syrup and lime juice.

2. Transfer to an ice cream maker and freeze according to manufacturer's instructions.

❧ Variations

Tart Key Lime Ice Cream: Reduce Simple Syrup to ½ cup (125 mL).

Margarita Ice Cream: Add 2 tbsp (25 mL) each tequila and orange-flavored liqueur to the machine in the last 5 minutes of freezing and let machine stir them in.

Key Lime Pie Ice Cream

Fans of the popular Florida dessert will want to try this because it's tart and creamy with a graham cracker crust blended right in.

3	eggs	3
1 cup	granulated sugar	250 mL
1 cup	whipping (35%) cream	250 mL
½ cup	milk	125 mL
½ cup	key lime juice	125 mL
½ cup	mini marshmallows	125 mL
3	graham crackers, broken into small pieces	3

1. In a bowl, whisk eggs with sugar until thickened and pale yellow. Set aside.

2. In a medium saucepan over medium-low heat, bring cream and milk to a simmer. Gradually whisk into the egg mixture.

3. Return entire mixture to the saucepan. Cook over low heat, stirring constantly, until the mixture is thick enough to coat the back of a wooden spoon. Be careful not to let it boil. Strain into a clean large bowl. Let cool to room temperature.

4. Stir in lime juice. Cover and refrigerate until completely cold or overnight.

5. Stir cream mixture. Transfer to an ice cream maker and freeze according to manufacturer's instructions.

6. Add marshmallows and graham crackers in the last 5 minutes of freezing and let machine stir them in.

Lemon Ice Cream

We like this at its most lemony, but you can cut back on the lemon if you prefer just a hint of citrus. This ice cream provides a wonderful background on which to explore different taste sensations (see Variations, right).

Serving suggestion: You will need an additional 6 lemons. Use these lemons as shells for the ice cream: Cut one-third off the top of each lemon. Set tops aside. Squeeze juice out of the bottoms, then scrape out any membranes. Scoop ice cream into shells. Top with lids. Freeze until ready to serve.

4	egg yolks	4
	Zest and juice of 2 lemons	
2 cups	whipping (35%) cream	500 mL
1 cup	milk	250 mL
⅔ cup	granulated sugar	150 mL

1. In a bowl, whisk egg yolks with lemon zest until pale yellow. Set aside.

2. In a medium saucepan over medium-low heat, bring cream, milk and sugar to a simmer, stirring constantly, until sugar is dissolved. Gradually whisk into the egg mixture.

3. Return entire mixture to the saucepan. Cook over low heat, stirring constantly, until the mixture is thick enough to coat the back of a wooden spoon. Be careful not to let it boil. Strain into a clean large bowl. Let cool to room temperature.

4. Stir in lemon juice. Cover and refrigerate until completely cold or overnight.

5. Stir cream mixture. Transfer to an ice cream maker and freeze according to manufacturer's instructions.

Variations

Add ¼ cup (50 mL) poppy seeds for a crunchy texture or ¼ cup (50 mL) mini-marshmallows for a mellow flavor. Another variation, inspired by a Danish friend's lemon pepper cookies, is to add 1 tbsp (15 mL) freshly ground black pepper. Add in the last 5 minutes of freezing and let machine stir them in.

Frozen Lemon Ginger Pie

This is a gourmet version of a classic ice cream pie. Gingersnaps are the perfect flavor to offset the pucker-worthy ice cream. Try serving it at your next dinner party; this pie is definitely a crowd pleaser.

- Preheat oven to 350°F (180°C)
- 10-inch (25 cm) glass pie plate or springform pan

Crust

1 1/2 cups	finely crushed gingersnap cookies	375 mL
1/2 cup	finely chopped crystallized ginger	125 mL
1/3 cup	unsalted butter	75 mL
2 tbsp	granulated sugar	25 mL

Ice Cream

3	egg yolks	3
1 cup	granulated sugar	250 mL
4 tsp	grated lemon zest	20 mL
2 cups	milk	500 mL
2 cups	whipping (35%) cream	500 mL
1 cup	freshly squeezed lemon juice	250 mL
	Lemon slices or shavings of dark chocolate	

1. *To make Crust:* In a bowl, combine gingersnap cookies, crystallized ginger, butter and sugar until crumbs are evenly moistened. Press evenly into pie plate. Bake in middle of preheated oven for 7 minutes or until firm to the touch. Let cool in pan on a rack.

2. *To make Ice Cream:* In a bowl, whisk egg yolks with sugar and lemon zest until thickened and pale yellow. Set aside.

3. In a medium saucepan over medium-low heat, bring milk to a simmer. Gradually whisk into the egg mixture.

4. Return entire mixture to the saucepan. Cook over low heat, stirring constantly, until the mixture is thick enough to coat the back of a wooden spoon. Be careful not to let it boil. Strain into a clean large bowl. Let cool to room temperature.

5. Stir in whipping cream and lemon juice. Cover and refrigerate until completely cold or overnight.

6. Stir cream mixture. Transfer to an ice cream maker and freeze according to manufacturer's instructions.

7. Spread ice cream evenly in crust and wrap pie plate in waxed paper or parchment paper. Freeze until firm, about 2 hours, or for up to 2 days.

8. Half an hour before serving, put pie plate in refrigerator to soften. Garnish with lemon slices or dark chocolate.

Tips: In a pinch, you can use graham crackers instead of the gingersnap cookies.

If using the springform pan, line the sides with waxed paper once the crust is cool.

❧ SERVES 8

Lemon Caramel Ice Cream

This ice cream requires a bit of swirling at the end to make it really special. We tried mixing the lemon flavor and the caramel together, but it just didn't wow the crowd. The swirling takes a bit of getting used to, but it's definitely worth it.

3	egg yolks	3
1 cup	granulated sugar	250 mL
4 tsp	grated lemon zest	20 mL
2 cups	milk	500 mL
2 cups	whipping (35%) cream	500 mL
1 cup	freshly squeezed lemon juice	250 mL
1 cup	store-bought caramel sauce	250 mL

1. In a bowl, whisk egg yolks with sugar and lemon zest until thickened and pale yellow. Set aside.

2. In a medium saucepan over medium-low heat, bring milk to a simmer. Gradually whisk into the egg mixture.

3. Return entire mixture to the saucepan. Cook over low heat, stirring constantly, until the mixture is thick enough to coat the back of a wooden spoon. Be careful not to let it boil. Strain into a clean large bowl. Let cool to room temperature.

4. Stir in whipping cream and lemon juice. Cover and refrigerate until completely cold or overnight.

5. Stir cream mixture. Transfer to an ice cream maker and freeze according to manufacturer's instructions.

6. Meanwhile, in a saucepan, heat caramel sauce until runny. Remove from heat.

7. In the last 5 minutes of freezing, using a spoon or a knife, drizzle caramel into the churning ice cream, creating a ribbon effect.

Lemon Dill Ice Cream

SERVES 6

Don't strain the dill out of the ice cream mixture. The result is a surprisingly delicious lemony custard frozen dessert that looks as good as it tastes. Pair it with ginger cookies to end a summer barbeque or with ginger cake for a sophisticated dinner party finale.

3	eggs	3
1 cup	granulated sugar, divided	250 mL
2 cups	whipping (35%) cream	500 mL
1 tbsp	grated lemon zest	15 mL
1 tbsp	finely chopped fresh dill	15 mL
1/3 cup	freshly squeezed lemon juice	75 mL

1. In a bowl, whisk egg yolks with 1/2 cup (125 mL) of the sugar until thickened and pale yellow. Set aside.

2. In a medium saucepan over medium-low heat, cook cream, the remaining 1/2 cup (125 mL) sugar and lemon zest, stirring, until sugar is dissolved. Gradually whisk into the egg mixture.

3. Return entire mixture to saucepan. Add dill and cook over low heat, stirring constantly, until the mixture is thick enough to coat the back of a wooden spoon. Be careful not to let it boil. Transfer to a clean large bowl. Let cool to room temperature. Cover and refrigerate until completely cold or overnight.

4. Stir cream mixture. Transfer to an ice cream maker and freeze according to manufacturer's instructions. At the semifrozen stage, add lemon juice in a slow, steady stream and continue freezing.

Lemon Poppy Seed Ice Cream

SERVES 8

Who can resist the flavor of a lemon poppy seed muffin? It's the perfect flavor combo — tart lemons mixed with crunchy poppy seeds. We thought this baking duo would translate perfectly into a refreshing ice cream, and we were right! Just make sure to add the poppy seeds at the very end of freezing, or they will get soggy and fall to the bottom.

Tip: Make sure not to dump the poppy seeds in all at once or they will clump together and will not distribute evenly.

3	egg yolks	3
1 cup	granulated sugar	250 mL
4 tsp	grated lemon zest	20 mL
2 cups	milk	500 mL
2 cups	whipping (35%) cream	500 mL
1 cup	freshly squeezed lemon juice	250 mL
½ cup	poppy seeds	125mL

1. In a bowl, whisk egg yolks with sugar and lemon zest until thickened and pale yellow. Set aside.

2. In a medium saucepan over medium-low heat, bring milk to a simmer. Gradually whisk into the egg mixture.

3. Return entire mixture to the saucepan. Cook over low heat, stirring constantly, until the mixture is thick enough to coat the back of a wooden spoon. Be careful not to let it boil. Strain into a clean large bowl. Let cool to room temperature.

4. Stir in whipping cream and lemon juice. Cover and refrigerate until completely cold or overnight.

5. Stir cream mixture. Transfer to an ice cream maker and freeze according to manufacturer's instructions. Add poppy seeds in the last 5 minutes of freezing and let machine stir them in.

Pucker-Up Ice Cream

SERVES 8

There's nothing more refreshing than a tall, cool glass of lemonade in the summertime, which is why we expanded on a lemon float to make this ice cream. The creaminess combined with tart, juicy lemons really makes your taste buds tingle.

Tip: Make sure to add the lemon and lime juice when the mixture is completely cold or the acid could curdle the cream mixture.

Serving suggestion: For a fabulous end to a dinner party, serve a scoop of Pucker-Up Ice Cream with a slice of lemon pound cake and a few fresh raspberries.

4	egg yolks	4
1 ¼ cups	granulated sugar	300 mL
2 cups	table (18%) cream	500 mL
2 cups	milk	500 mL
	Zest of 2 lemons	
½ cup	freshly squeezed lemon juice	125 mL
	Zest of 1 lime	
¼ cup	freshly squeezed lime juice	50 mL

1. In a bowl, whisk egg yolks with sugar until thickened and pale yellow. Set aside.

2. In a medium saucepan over medium-low heat, bring cream and milk to a simmer. Gradually whisk into the egg mixture.

3. Return entire mixture to the saucepan. Cook over low heat, stirring constantly, until mixture is thick enough to coat the back of a wooden spoon. Be careful not to let it boil. Strain into a clean large bowl. Let cool to room temperature. Cover and refrigerate until completely cold or overnight.

4. Stir in lemon zest and juice and lime zest and juice (see Tip, left). Transfer to an ice cream maker and freeze according to manufacturer's instructions.

Variations

Grapefruit Pucker-Up Ice Cream: Substitute zest of 1 grapefruit and ¾ cup (175 mL) grapefruit juice for the lemon and lime zest and juice.

Lime Pucker-Up Ice Cream: Omit lemon zest and juice and increase lime zest to 3 limes and juice to ¾ cup (175 mL).

Watermelon Ice Cream

Watermelon is traditionally made into an ice, but we thought it would be just as good as an ice cream. The chocolate chunks pop out against the pink ice cream, mimicking the actual fruit.

6 cups	cubed watermelon	750 mL
2	egg yolks	2
1 cup	granulated sugar	250 mL
2 cups	milk	500 mL
2 cups	whipping (35%) cream	500 mL
1 cup	semisweet chocolate chunks	250 mL

1. In a food processor, purée watermelon until it is a thick liquid. Set aside.

2. In a bowl, whisk egg yolks with sugar until thickened and pale yellow. Set aside.

3. In a medium saucepan over medium-low heat, bring milk to a simmer. Gradually whisk into the egg mixture.

4. Return entire mixture to the saucepan. Cook over low heat, stirring constantly, until the mixture is thick enough to coat the back of a wooden spoon. Be careful not to let it boil. Strain into a clean large bowl. Let cool to room temperature.

5. Stir in watermelon purée and whipping cream. Cover and refrigerate until completely cold or overnight.

6. Stir cream mixture. Transfer to ice cream maker and freeze according to manufacturer's instructions. Add chocolate chunks in the last 5 minutes of freezing and let machine stir them in.

Apricot Ice Cream

We recommend using canned apricots, but you can also use fresh ones that have been peeled and pitted. The addition of dried apricots, however, is important, because it amplifies the flavor.

Tip: For an extra-fruity version, you can finely chop your favorite fruit leather and add it in the last 5 minutes of freezing.

Serving suggestion: Although Apricot Ice Cream is satisfying on its own, when scooped into a chocolate cup it's transformed into a dinner party dazzler. Chocolate cups are available in supermarkets. Their small, cup-like shapes make for elegant desserts.

½ cup	chopped dried apricots	125 mL
½ cup	Simple Syrup (see recipe, page 20)	125 mL
2	cans (each 14 oz/398 mL) apricots in syrup	2
1 tbsp	freshly squeezed lemon juice	15 mL
1 cup	whipping (35%) cream	250 mL

1. In a small bowl, combine dried apricots and syrup. Let soak for 15 minutes.

2. In a food processor or blender, purée dried apricot mixture, canned apricots with syrup and lemon juice until smooth.

3. Transfer to a clean large bowl. Stir in cream.

4. Stir cream mixture. Transfer to an ice cream maker and freeze according to manufacturer's instructions.

Variation
Prune Ice Cream: Substitute 1 cup (250 mL) pitted dried prunes soaked in the Simple Syrup for both the dried apricots and canned apricots.

Peach Ice Cream

This ice cream is the perfect accompaniment to a home-baked peach pie. The recipe calls for fresh peaches, but if you crave it out of season, 1 can (14 oz/398 mL) peaches, drained, will do just fine.

Tip: This is a good crisper cleaner, especially during the last days of summer, when you have an assortment of fruits in the refrigerator. Fruits such as peaches, plums, strawberries and raspberries are perfect for this. (Apples wouldn't work.) The juicier the peaches, the better.

4	peaches, peeled and pitted	4
2 tbsp	freshly squeezed lime juice	25 mL
6	egg yolks	6
⅔ cup	granulated sugar	150 mL
1½ cups	table (18%) cream	375 mL
1½ cups	milk	375 mL
1 tbsp	vanilla	15 mL

1. In a food processor or blender, purée peaches with lime juice until smooth. Push purée through a fine sieve to remove any tough pieces of skin. Set aside.

2. In a bowl, whisk egg yolks with sugar until thickened and pale yellow. Set aside.

3. In a medium saucepan over medium-low heat, bring cream and milk to a simmer. Gradually whisk into the egg mixture.

4. Return entire mixture to the saucepan. Cook over low heat, stirring constantly, until the mixture is thick enough to coat the back of a wooden spoon. Be careful not to let it boil. Strain into a clean large bowl. Let cool to room temperature.

5. Stir in peach purée and vanilla. Cover and refrigerate until completely cold or overnight.

6. Stir cream mixture. Transfer to an ice cream maker and freeze according to manufacturer's instructions.

❧ Variation

Cardamom Peach Ice Cream: Add 1 tsp (5 mL) ground cardamom to hot strained cream mixture.

Blackberry-Peach Ice Cream: Add 1 cup (250 mL) blackberries to food processor along with peaches and lime juice.

Peach Melba Ice Cream

SERVES 6 TO 8

Peaches and raspberries, the foundation of this fabulous dessert — named after the Australian opera star Nellie Melba — are terrific swirled into an ice cream base.

Tip: You may want to make this when fresh raspberries and peaches are not available. If so, substitute 1 can (14 oz/ 398 mL) sliced peaches, drained, and an additional ¼ cup (50 mL) raspberry jam mixed with the orange juice.

Serving suggestion: For a spectacular finish to a dinner party, serve this sparkler. In a food processor or blender, purée 1 cup (250 mL) chopped pitted peeled fresh peaches with 1 cup (250 mL) fresh raspberries. Divide purée among champagne glasses. Add 1 scoop of Peach Melba Ice Cream or store-bought raspberry sherbet. Top with sparkling wine and a sprig of fresh mint.

3	ripe peaches, peeled, pitted and chopped	3
1 cup	Simple Syrup (see recipe, page 20)	250 mL
1 cup	whipping (35%) cream	250 mL
1 cup	milk	250 mL
1 cup	fresh raspberries	250 mL
¼ cup	raspberry jam	50 mL
¼ cup	orange juice	50 mL

1. In a food processor or blender, purée peaches with syrup until smooth. Transfer to a clean large bowl. Stir in cream and milk. Cover and refrigerate until completely cold or overnight.

2. Stir cream mixture. Transfer to an ice cream maker and freeze according to manufacturer's instructions.

3. Meanwhile, in a food processor or blender, purée raspberries, jam and orange juice until smooth.

4. When the ice cream is almost frozen, pack half of it into a freezerproof container. Spoon in half of the raspberry mixture. Repeat layers once.

5. Gently swirl raspberry mixture into ice cream with a knife. Cover and freeze until firm.

Mango Ice Cream Brûlée

SERVES 6

A crunchy, sugary brûlée topping lends an elegant touch to this rich, tropical treat.

Tips: For a more pronounced mango flavor, use 3 mangos.

If you don't have a butane or propane torch, place ramekins on a baking sheet and broil until sugar bubbles and changes color. Watch constantly and rotate ramekins as necessary.

1	vanilla bean	1
1½ cups	milk, divided	375 mL
1 cup	whipping (35%) cream	250 mL
4	egg yolks	4
2	ripe mangos, peeled and chopped	2
½ cup	granulated sugar	125 mL
Pinch	salt	Pinch
6 tbsp	turbinado sugar (such as Sugar in the Raw)	90 mL

1. Slit vanilla bean lengthwise and scrape seeds into a medium saucepan. Add vanilla pod, ½ cup (125 mL) of the milk and the cream. Bring to a simmer over medium-low heat. Remove from heat and let stand for 15 minutes, allowing the flavor of the vanilla to infuse. Remove and discard vanilla pod.

2. Meanwhile, in a food processor or blender, purée egg yolks, mangos, the remaining 1 cup (250 mL) milk, sugar and salt until smooth. Transfer to a bowl and whisk in the vanilla mixture.

3. Return entire mixture to the saucepan. Cook over low heat, stirring constantly, until the mixture is thick enough to coat the back of a wooden spoon. Be careful not to let it boil. Strain into a clean large bowl. Let cool to room temperature. Cover and refrigerate until completely cold or overnight.

4. Stir cream mixture. Transfer to an ice cream maker and freeze according to manufacturer's instructions.

5. While ice cream is still a bit runny, transfer to six ½-cup (125 mL) ramekins, tapping on counter to remove any air. Cover each ramekin with plastic wrap and store in the freezer, making sure they're flat.

6. Just before you're ready to serve, remove ramekins from freezer and sprinkle each with 1 tbsp (15 mL) turbinado sugar. Using a butane or propane torch, heat the sugar until it bubbles and changes color.

Mango-Mascarpone Ice Cream

This easy-to-make, easy-to-like ice cream combines a mild, soft Italian cheese with tropical fruit. The banana gives it a special smoothness. For a slightly lighter version, substitute whole milk for the whipping cream.

Serving suggestion:
You can easily make a party-size ice cream cake at home. Slice one store-bought loaf cake (preferably a 9- by 5-inch/ 23 by 13 cm lemon pound cake) horizontally into thirds. Line a 9- by 5-inch (2 L) loaf pan with plastic wrap. Place the bottom cake layer in the pan. Spread layer of softened ice cream 1/2 inch (1 cm) deep over top. Repeat layers once. Top with remaining cake layer. Wrap with plastic wrap and freeze until firm. A few minutes before serving, cut into 2-inch (5 cm) slices. Serve with fresh fruit.

1	mango, peeled and cut into chunks (about 1 1/2 cups/375 mL)	1
1	large ripe banana, sliced	1
1/2 cup	Simple Syrup (see recipe, page 20)	125 mL
1/2 cup	mascarpone cheese	125 mL
1/2 cup	whipping (35%) cream	125 mL
1 tbsp	lime zest	15 mL
1 tbsp	freshly squeezed lime juice	15 mL

1. In a food processor or blender, purée mango, banana, syrup and mascarpone cheese until smooth.

2. Transfer to a bowl. Stir in cream and lime zest and juice.

3. Transfer to an ice cream maker and freeze according to manufacturer's instructions.

❧ Variation
Fudgy Mango-Mascarpone Ice Cream: Because mango and chocolate are an unbeatable combo, try combining the two. Add 1/2 cup (125 mL) chopped chocolate fudge in the last 5 minutes of freezing and let machine stir it in.

Mango–Sour Cream Ice Cream

For a very easy and very good dessert, this can't be beat. The beautiful orange color looks as good as the dessert tastes. For a more intense flavor, add 1 more mango.

Tip: This ice cream will be soft. For firmer ice cream, place in the freezer for at least 2 hours.

Serving suggestion: This is a wonderful ice cream to bring out the flavors of a simple yet spectacular tropical fruit plate. Arrange long, thin slices of peeled mangos, melons and papayas on dessert plates. Place a scoop of Mango–Sour Cream Ice Cream on each. Top each with a thin slice of star fruit.

1	mango, peeled and chopped (about 1 1/2 cups/375 mL)	1
	Juice of 1 lime	
3/4 cup	granulated sugar	175 mL
1 1/2 cups	sour cream	375 mL

1. In a food processor or blender, purée mango, lime juice and sugar until smooth.

2. Transfer to a bowl. Stir in sour cream. Cover and refrigerate until completely cold or overnight.

3. Transfer to an ice cream maker and freeze according to manufacturer's instructions.

Avocado Ice Cream

This popular South American dessert promises not only a beautiful color but also a velvety texture. Make sure you use the ripest avocados you can find. Treat this as an adventure in flavor and complement it with a scoop of traditional vanilla or chocolate ice cream.

Serving suggestion: Melon ballers, available in various sizes, are very handy for serving small scoops of ice cream (which may be appealing after a large dinner). Pile small scoops of a single flavor in a bowl or present a variety of different flavors on an ice cream tasting plate.

4	ripe avocados, peeled, pitted and chopped (about 2 cups/500 mL)	4
1 cup	whipping (35%) cream	250 mL
½ cup	granulated sugar	125 mL
¼ cup	freshly squeezed lime juice	50 mL

1. In a food processor or blender, purée avocados, cream, sugar and lime juice until smooth.

2. Transfer to an ice cream maker and freeze according to manufacturer's instructions.

Avocado Lime Ice Cream

This super-simple dessert is the sweetest way to use avocados. For an elegant presentation, top with candied lime zest (see recipe, page 97).

Tip: For more zing, try adding 1 or 2 chopped jalapeño peppers with the avocados.

3	ripe avocados, peeled and pitted	3
1½ cups	milk	375 mL
½ cup	granulated sugar	125 mL
	Grated zest and juice of 1 lime	
1 cup	whipping (35%) cream	250 mL

1. In a food processor or blender, purée avocados, milk, sugar, lime zest and lime juice until smooth.

2. Pour into a bowl and whisk in cream. Cover and refrigerate until completely cold or overnight.

3. Stir cream mixture. Transfer to an ice cream maker and freeze according to manufacturer's instructions.

Honey, Lemon and Thyme Ice Cream (page 60)

Raspberry-Blackberry Ice Cream (page 66)

Lemon Caramel Ice Cream (page 84)

Strawberries and Cream Ice Cream (page 67)

Candied Lime Zest

This garnish is easy to make and can be used to decorate any dessert, from the Avocado Lime Ice Cream (see recipe, page 96) to a plain custard, crème brûlée or chocolate cake.

| 2 | limes | 2 |
| 1 cup | granulated sugar | 250 mL |

1. Slice zest from limes in long, thin strips, being careful not to take too much of the white part.

2. Bring a small saucepan of water to a boil and blanch the zest for 1 to 2 minutes. Drain zest, discarding water. Repeat with fresh boiling water. Drain zest on a paper towel.

3. In a small saucepan over medium-low heat, bring sugar and 1 cup (250 mL) of water to a simmer. Cook, stirring, until sugar is completely dissolved. Add zest and simmer for 3 to 4 minutes, or until bubbly. Transfer to parchment paper and let cool.

❧ MAKES ABOUT 2 CUPS (500 mL)

Banana Ice Cream

SERVES 6

Use the ripest bananas you can find for this recipe. It's luscious on its own but even more decadent with ½ cup (125 mL) toasted chopped pecans or walnuts added in the last 5 minutes of freezing.

Tip: If you have a real sweet tooth, you can increase the sugar to ⅔ cup (150 mL).

Serving suggestions:
For bananaholics, serve a scoop of Banana Ice Cream on a bed of sliced bananas. Top with whipped cream, chocolate sauce and a maraschino cherry. Or (for adults only) splash on a bit of banana liqueur.

2	eggs	2
½ cup	granulated sugar	125 mL
1 tbsp	all-purpose flour	15 mL
1 ½ cups	table (18%) cream	375 mL
3	large ripe bananas	3
¼ cup	milk	50 mL
1 tsp	freshly squeezed lemon juice	5 mL
1 tsp	vanilla	5 mL

1. In a bowl, whisk eggs with sugar until thickened and pale yellow. Whisk in flour. Set aside.

2. In a medium saucepan over medium-low heat, bring cream to a simmer. Gradually whisk into the egg mixture.

3. Return entire mixture to the saucepan. Cook over low heat, stirring constantly, until the mixture is thick enough to coat the back of a wooden spoon. Be careful not to let it boil. Strain into a clean large bowl. Let cool to room temperature.

4. In a food processor or blender, purée bananas with milk until smooth. Pour into cream mixture, scraping down the side of the bowl. Stir in lemon juice and vanilla. Cover and refrigerate until completely cold or overnight.

5. Stir cream mixture. Transfer to an ice cream maker and freeze according to manufacturer's instructions.

❧ Variation
Banana Mocha Ice Cream: Add ½ cup (125 mL) shaved chocolate in the last 5 minutes of freezing. For a touch of coffee, add ¼ cup (50 mL) chocolate-covered espresso beans in the last 5 minutes of freezing.

Spiced Banana Ice Cream

Star anise is the dominant flavor in Chinese five-spice powder, and cardamom pods can often be found in East Indian dishes. Play with the spice proportions to create your own signature recipe.

3	egg yolks	3
1/2	vanilla bean	1/2
10	cardamom pods (bruised)	10
2	star anise pods	2
1 1/2 cups	whipping (35%) cream	375 mL
1 1/2 cups	milk	375 mL
3/4 cup	packed brown sugar	175 mL
1/2 tsp	ground nutmeg	2 mL
1/2 tsp	ground cinnamon	2 mL
Pinch	freshly ground white pepper	Pinch
2	ripe bananas, puréed (about 3/4 cup/175 mL)	2

1. In a bowl, whisk egg yolks until pale yellow. Set aside.

2. Slit vanilla bean lengthwise and scrape seeds into a medium saucepan. Add vanilla pod, cardamom, star anise, cream, milk, brown sugar, nutmeg, cinnamon and white pepper. Place the saucepan over medium-low heat and bring to a simmer. Remove from heat, cover and let stand for 30 minutes, allowing the spices to infuse the cream.

3. Remove and discard vanilla pod. Bring mixture to a simmer over low heat. Gradually whisk into the egg yolks.

4. Return entire mixture to the saucepan. Cook over low heat, stirring constantly, until the mixture is thick enough to coat the back of a wooden spoon. Be careful not to let it boil. Strain into a clean large bowl. Let cool to room temperature.

5. Stir in puréed bananas. Cover and refrigerate until completely cold or overnight.

6. Stir cream mixture. Transfer to an ice cream maker and freeze according to manufacturer's instructions.

Banana Toffee Ice Cream

This ice cream features an unbeatable combination that's favored by our Scottish friends, who call it "banoffee ice cream." You can use your favorite brand of chewy or hard toffee for this recipe. Sweetened condensed milk gives it a cheesecake-like flavor.

Tip: This ice cream will be soft. For firmer ice cream, place in the freezer for at least 2 hours.

If you plan to serve this recipe to small children, either leave out the toffee (because it's too sharp and can cause choking) or substitute the same amount of butterscotch chips for it.

3	large ripe bananas	3
	Juice of 1 lemon	
1	can (10 oz/300 mL) sweetened condensed milk	1
1⅓ cups	whipping (35%) cream	325 mL
2	packages (each 4 oz/112 g) toffee, chopped into ¼-inch (0.5 cm) squares	2

1. In a food processor or blender, purée bananas until smooth. Add lemon juice and sweetened condensed milk. Process until combined.

2. Transfer to a clean large bowl. Stir in cream. Cover and refrigerate until completely cold or overnight.

3. Stir cream mixture. Transfer to an ice cream maker and freeze according to manufacturer's instructions. Add toffee in the last 5 minutes of freezing and let machine stir it in.

✽ Variation

Banana Chocolate Toffee Ice Cream: For extra texture, add ¼ cup (50 mL) chocolate chips.

Coconut Ice Cream

We love the stark white color of this rich dessert, but you can add a little color by toasting the coconut flakes first. Although we call for a 15-oz (426 mL) can of coconut cream, your store may only stock 14-oz (398 mL) cans. As long as the difference in size is no more than 1 oz (30 mL), the recipe should turn out just fine. Don't confuse coconut cream, which is thick and sweetened, with coconut milk, which is thinner and unsweetened.

Tip: To toast coconut, spread the coconut in a thin layer in a metal cake pan or on a rimmed baking sheet. Toast in 350°F (180°C) oven, watching carefully to prevent burning or overbrowning, for 3 to 5 minutes or until golden and fragrant. Let cool to room temperature.

1	can (15 oz/426 mL) coconut cream (see Introduction, left)	1
1½ cups	whipping (35%) cream	375 mL
1 cup	milk	250 mL
½ cup	sweetened flaked coconut (see Tip, left)	125 mL

1. In a food processor or blender, purée coconut cream, whipping cream, milk and flaked coconut until thoroughly blended.

2. Transfer to an ice cream maker and freeze according to manufacturer's instructions.

❧ Variation

Thai Coconut Lemongrass Ice Cream: For a fragrant, Thai-inspired dessert, infuse the coconut with lemongrass. Cut 4 stalks lemongrass in half lengthwise. Using a mallet, meat pounder, rolling pin or hammer, pound the stalks a few times to release their flavor. In a medium saucepan, bring coconut cream and lemongrass to a boil. Remove from heat and let stand for 30 minutes. Remove lemongrass stalks and proceed with recipe.

Coconut Mango Ice Cream

This exotic ice cream with the color of a gorgeous sunset requires no fuss to prepare. You can use fresh ripe mango or sliced mango from a can. Either way, place in a food processor or blender and purée until smooth.

Tip: Puréed fresh mango can be stringy. For a smoother texture, press mango through a sieve before measuring.

1	can (14 oz/398 mL) coconut cream (see Introduction, page 101)	1
2 cups	puréed mango (see Tip, left)	500 mL
½ cup	milk	125 mL
½ cup	table (18%) cream	125 mL

1. In a bowl, stir together coconut cream, mango, milk and cream until combined.

2. Transfer to an ice cream maker and freeze according to manufacturer's instructions.

Variation

Coconut Cream Pie: Add 1 cup (250 mL) crumbled graham crackers to the ice cream maker in the last 5 minutes of freezing and let the machine stir them in. Serve topped with toasted coconut and a sprinkling of fleur de sel.

Tropical Ice Cream

Take your taste buds on a trip to the tropics with this coconut ice cream flavored with grated ginger and fresh lime juice. You won't believe this tangy dessert is made from pure unsweetened coconut milk — and the best part is that there is no cooking required.

Tip: Because there is no cooking in this recipe, you can go straight to the ice cream maker if you use chilled coconut milk and cream.

Serving suggestions: Slice fresh kiwifruit, limes, mangos and papaya to garnish two scoops of ice cream. Top with a piece of crystallized ginger.

2	cans (each 14 oz/398 mL) unsweetened coconut milk	2
1 cup	granulated sugar	250 mL
1 cup	half-and-half (10%) cream	250 mL
	Zest of 1 lime	
1/3 cup	freshly squeezed lime juice	75 mL
1/3 cup	grated gingerroot	75 mL

1. In a bowl, whisk together coconut milk, sugar, half-and-half, lime zest and juice and ginger until sugar is dissolved and mixture is smooth.

2. Cover and refrigerate until completely cold or overnight.

3. Stir cream mixture. Transfer to an ice cream maker and freeze according to manufacturer's instructions.

Fig Chutney Ice Cream

Plump dried figs give a more satisfying and intense flavor to this ice cream than do fresh figs. Enjoy this as an ending to a meal of simply prepared grilled meat, such as barbecued lamb.

Serving suggestion: Serve with sliced fresh mangos.

1	large banana, sliced	1
6	dried figs, finely chopped	6
½ cup	Simple Syrup (see recipe, page 20)	125 mL
1 cup	whipping (35%) cream	250 mL
1 cup	milk	250 mL
1 tsp	mango chutney	5 mL
¼ tsp	vanilla	1 mL

1. In a food processor or blender, purée banana, figs and syrup until smooth.

2. Transfer to a large bowl. Stir in cream, milk, chutney and vanilla.

3. Transfer to an ice cream maker and freeze according to manufacturer's instructions.

Rum Raisin Ice Cream

Use plump golden raisins and premium rum. Serve on its own or as a complement to bananas sautéed with brown sugar and butter.

1 ½ cups	golden raisins	375 mL
⅓ cup	orange juice	75 mL
2	eggs	2
¾ cup	packed light brown sugar	175 mL
1 cup	half-and-half (10%) cream	250 mL
1 cup	whipping (35%) cream	250 mL
¼ cup	dark rum	50 mL

1. In a bowl, toss raisins with orange juice. Let stand for 1 hour.

2. Meanwhile, in a separate bowl, whisk eggs with brown sugar until thickened and pale yellow. Set aside.

3. In a medium saucepan over medium-low heat, bring half-and-half and whipping cream to a simmer. Gradually whisk into the egg mixture.

4. Return entire mixture to the saucepan. Cook over low heat, stirring constantly, until the mixture is thick enough to coat the back of a wooden spoon. Be careful not to let it boil. Strain into a clean large bowl. Let cool to room temperature.

5. Stir in raisin mixture and rum. Cover and refrigerate until completely cold or overnight.

6. Stir cream mixture. Transfer to an ice cream maker and freeze according to manufacturer's instructions.

Tutti-Frutti Ice Cream

SERVES 6 TO 8

Any or all of the candied fruits of your choosing can be added to this rich vanilla base. For a truly Christmasy dessert, serve with a slice of your favorite fruitcake. Or toss a few slices of fruitcake, crumbled, into the ice cream in the last 5 minutes of freezing.

Tips: This ice cream will be soft. For firmer ice cream, place in the freezer for at least 2 hours.

We have used 2% milk here and in several other recipes. Not only does it reduce the fat content, but it tastes just as good as whole milk. If you prefer a full-fat version, use whole milk instead.

3	egg yolks	3
1/3 cup	superfine sugar	75 mL
1	vanilla bean	1
1 1/2 cups	2% milk (see Tip, left)	375 mL
1 1/2 cups	whipping (35%) cream	375 mL
1 1/4 cups	chopped mixed candied fruit (such as green and red cherries, pineapple, mango, papaya, lime peel and/or orange peel)	300 mL

1. In a bowl, whisk egg yolks with sugar until thickened and pale yellow. Set aside.

2. Slit vanilla bean lengthwise and scrape seeds into a medium saucepan. Add vanilla pod, milk and cream. Place the saucepan over medium-low heat and bring just to a simmer. Remove from heat. Let stand for 15 minutes, allowing the flavor of the vanilla to infuse.

3. Discard pod. Bring mixture to a simmer over medium-low heat and simmer for 5 minutes. Gradually whisk into the egg mixture.

4. Return entire mixture to the saucepan. Cook over low heat, stirring constantly, until the mixture is thick enough to coat the back of a wooden spoon. Be careful not to let it boil. Strain into a clean large bowl. Let cool to room temperature. Cover and refrigerate until completely cold or overnight.

5. Stir cream mixture. Transfer to an ice cream maker and freeze according to manufacturer's instructions. Add candied fruit in the last 5 minutes of freezing and let machine stir it in.

Nutty
Ice Creams

Nut Brittle Ice Cream

SERVES 6 TO 8

A yummy variety of nuts goes into this praline, which is best added at the very end of the ice cream maker's work.

Tip: We have used 2% milk here and in several other recipes. Not only does it reduce the fat content, but it tastes just as good as whole milk. If you prefer a full-fat version, use whole milk instead.

3	egg yolks	3
1 cup	granulated sugar, divided	250 mL
1 1/2 cups	2% milk (see Tip, left)	375 mL
1 tbsp	vegetable oil	15 mL
1/2 cup	macadamia nuts, broken into halves	125 mL
1/2 cup	hazelnuts, toasted, skinned and chopped (see Tip, right)	125 mL
1/2 cup	sliced almonds	125 mL
1 1/2 cups	whipping (35%) cream	375 mL
2 tsp	vanilla	10 mL

1. In a bowl, whisk egg yolks with 6 tbsp (90 mL) sugar until thickened and pale yellow. Set aside.

2. In a medium saucepan over medium-low heat, bring milk to a simmer. Gradually whisk into the egg mixture.

3. Return entire mixture to the saucepan. Cook over low heat, stirring constantly, until the mixture is thick enough to coat the back of a wooden spoon. Be careful not to let it boil. Strain into a clean large bowl. Let cool to room temperature.

4. Meanwhile, brush a baking sheet with vegetable oil. In a medium saucepan over medium-low heat, stir together remaining sugar, macadamia nuts, hazelnuts, almonds and 1/4 cup (50 mL) water. Cook, without stirring, until sugar is dissolved. Increase heat to medium-high and boil for 3 to 5 minutes or until sugar turns golden brown and syrupy. Working quickly, pour and spread onto prepared baking sheet. Let cool until hard.

Tips: This ice cream will be soft. For firmer ice cream, place in the freezer for at least 2 hours.

To toast hazelnuts, place on a baking sheet in 300°F (150°C) oven until just toasted. When cool, rub toasted hazelnuts in a clean dish towel to remove skins.

5. Stir whipping cream and vanilla into milk mixture. Cover and refrigerate until completely cold or overnight.

6. Stir cream mixture. Transfer to an ice cream maker and freeze according to manufacturer's instructions.

7. Smash about three-quarters of the nut brittle into bite-size pieces. Add in the last 5 minutes of freezing and let machine stir them in.

8. Garnish each serving with some of the remaining nut brittle.

Cashew Ice Cream

2	eggs	2
1½ cups	2% milk (see Tip, page 108)	375 mL
1 cup	whipping (35%) cream	250 mL
¾ cup	Simple Syrup (see recipe, page 20)	175 mL
1 tsp	orange zest	5 mL
¼ tsp	vanilla	1 mL
1 cup	finely chopped unsalted cashews, toasted (see Tip, left)	250 mL

SERVES 6

This rich, buttery ice cream is luxuriously sweet and nutty. For a little variety, add 2 tbsp (25 mL) each sunflower seeds, raisins and chopped dates to the machine in the last 5 minutes of freezing.

Tip: To toast nuts, spread them in a thin layer in a metal cake pan or on a rimmed baking sheet. Toast in 350°F (180°C) oven, watching carefully to prevent burning or overbrowning, for 3 to 5 minutes or until golden and fragrant. Let cool to room temperature.

Serving suggestion: Give this ice cream a fiery bite with the following topping. Toss together ¼ cup (50 mL) unsalted cashews, 2 tbsp (25 mL) corn syrup and ¼ tsp (1 mL) cayenne pepper. Spread on a rimmed baking sheet. Bake in 350°F (180°C) oven for 5 minutes or until golden. Let cool. Chop and sprinkle over ice cream.

1. In a large bowl, whisk eggs until pale yellow. Set aside.

2. In a medium saucepan over medium-low heat, bring milk and cream to a simmer. Gradually whisk into the eggs.

3. Return entire mixture to the saucepan. Cook over low heat, stirring constantly, until the mixture is thick enough to coat the back of a wooden spoon. Be careful not to let it boil. Strain into a clean large bowl. Let cool to room temperature.

4. Stir in syrup, orange zest and vanilla. Cover and refrigerate until completely cold or overnight.

5. Stir cream mixture. Transfer to an ice cream maker and freeze according to manufacturer's instructions. Add cashews in the last 5 minutes of freezing.

❧ Variation

Cashew Raisin Ice Cream: Decrease cashews to ½ cup (125 mL) and add ½ cup (125 mL) golden raisins to the chilled cream mixture.

Chestnut Ice Cream

Chestnut purée can be found in gourmet food shops and some supermarkets in the imported foods section. If the purée doesn't have vanilla added, add 1 tsp (5 mL) vanilla to the recipe before you refrigerate.

Tip: This ice cream will be soft. For firmer ice cream, place in the freezer for at least 2 hours.

Chestnut purée comes in a 22 oz (675 mL) can. Leftovers are great as a dessert crêpe filling.

3	egg yolks	3
1/3 cup	granulated sugar	75 mL
1 cup	2% milk (see Tip, page 108)	250 mL
1 cup	table (18%) cream	250 mL
1 1/4 cups	unsweetened chestnut purée with vanilla added (see Tips, left)	300 mL
1 cup	whipping (35%) cream	250 mL
Pinch	salt	Pinch

1. In a bowl, whisk egg yolks with sugar until thickened and pale yellow. Set aside.

2. In a medium saucepan over medium-low heat, bring milk and table cream to a simmer. Stir in chestnut purée. Gradually whisk into the egg mixture.

3. Return entire mixture to the saucepan. Cook over low heat, stirring constantly, until the mixture is thick enough to coat the back of a wooden spoon. Be careful not to let it boil. Strain into a clean large bowl. Let cool to room temperature.

4. Stir in whipping cream and salt. Cover and refrigerate until completely cold or overnight.

5. Stir cream mixture. Transfer to an ice cream maker and freeze according to manufacturer's instructions.

Hazelnut Ice Cream

If you have a hankering for a hazelnut latte, you'll love the taste of this ice cream. Made with both hazelnut syrup and real nuts, this dessert is definitely for filbert fans!

2	eggs	2
2 cups	milk	500 mL
2 cups	whipping (35%) cream	500 mL
½ cup	hazelnut syrup (with sugar added)	125 mL
½ cup	hazelnuts	125 mL
½ cup	finely chopped chocolate (optional)	125 mL

1. In a bowl, whisk egg yolks until pale yellow. Set aside.

2. In a medium saucepan over medium-low heat, bring milk to a simmer. Gradually whisk into the egg mixture.

3. Return entire mixture to the saucepan. Cook over low heat, stirring constantly, until the mixture is thick enough to coat the back of a wooden spoon. Be careful not to let it boil. Strain into a clean large bowl. Let cool to room temperature.

4. Stir in whipping cream and hazelnut syrup. Cover and refrigerate until completely cold or overnight.

5. Place hazelnuts in a large plastic freezer bag and seal. Using a rolling pin or meat hammer, pound nuts into tiny pieces. Set aside.

6. Stir cream mixture. Transfer to an ice cream maker and freeze according to manufacturer's instructions. Add hazelnuts and chocolate (if using) in the last 5 minutes of freezing and let machine stir them in.

Hazelnut Honey Ice Cream

SERVES 4

Toasting the hazelnuts enhances their flavor in this delectable, rich dessert. Use clover or orange-blossom honey for optimum flavor.

Serving suggestion:
Drizzle a little more orange-blossom honey over each serving.

1 cup	hazelnuts	250 mL
4	egg yolks	4
⅓ cup	liquid honey	75 mL
½	vanilla bean	½
1 cup	milk	250 mL
½ cup	whipping (35%) cream	125 mL

1. Spread hazelnuts on rimmed baking sheet. Toast in a 350°F (180°C) oven, watching carefully to prevent burning or overbrowning, for about 5 minutes or until fragrant. Transfer to two clean dish towels and rub until the skins slip off. Chop finely and set aside.

2. In a bowl, whisk egg yolks with honey until thickened and pale yellow. Set aside.

3. Slit vanilla bean lengthwise and scrape seeds into a medium saucepan. Add vanilla pod, milk and cream. Place saucepan over medium-low heat and bring just to a simmer. Remove from heat. Let stand for 15 minutes, allowing the flavor of the vanilla to infuse.

4. Discard pod. Bring mixture to a simmer over medium-low heat and simmer for 5 minutes. Gradually whisk into the egg mixture.

5. Return entire mixture to the saucepan. Cook over low heat, stirring constantly, until the mixture is thick enough to coat the back of a wooden spoon. Be careful not to let it boil. Let cool to room temperature. Cover and refrigerate until completely cold or overnight.

6. Stir cream mixture. Transfer to an ice cream maker and freeze according to manufacturer's instructions. Add hazelnuts in the last 5 minutes of freezing and let machine stir them in.

Butter Pecan Ice Cream

You say pe-can, we say pe-cahn. However you pronounce it, this recipe is a classic. For extra crunchiness, toast the pecans before adding to the mixture.

Tip: This ice cream will be soft. For firmer ice cream, place in the freezer for at least 2 hours.

Serving suggestions: For an elegant finish to a barbecue, sandwich a scoop of Butter Pecan Ice Cream between two flat cookies (preferably chocolate chip) and freeze until firm. Although most cookies are flat, it is better to make ice cream sandwiches with flat, wide cookies instead of small, domed ones. Or spoon a simple caramel sauce over a scoop.

2	eggs	2
¼ cup	unsalted butter	50 mL
1 cup	packed brown sugar	250 mL
1 cup	table (18%) cream	250 mL
½ cup	milk	125 mL
1 cup	whipping (35%) cream	250 mL
1 tsp	vanilla	5 mL
¼ tsp	almond extract	1 mL
1 ½ cups	pecan halves	375 mL

1. In a bowl, whisk eggs until pale yellow. Set aside.

2. In a medium saucepan over medium heat, melt butter. Cook, stirring, until it begins to brown and smell slightly nutty. Add brown sugar. Stir until melted. Reduce heat to low. Add table cream and milk and bring to a simmer. Gradually whisk into the eggs.

3. Return entire mixture to the saucepan. Cook over low heat, stirring constantly, until the mixture is thick enough to coat the back of a wooden spoon. Be careful not to let it boil. Strain into a clean large bowl. Let cool to room temperature.

4. Stir in whipping cream, vanilla and almond extract. Cover and refrigerate until completely cold or overnight.

5. Stir cream mixture. Transfer to an ice cream maker and freeze according to manufacturer's instructions.

6. Add pecans in the last 5 minutes of freezing and let machine stir them in.

Pine Nut and Honey Ice Cream

SERVES 6

These two flavors make for an intense-tasting ice cream that will add a splash of elegance to your next dinner party. A dainty but crunchy cookie will work well on the side.

- Preheat oven to 400°F (200°C)
- Baking sheet

1 cup	pine nuts	250 mL
2	eggs	2
½ cup	liquid honey	125 mL
1 tbsp	granulated sugar	15 mL
Pinch	salt	Pinch
1 cup	milk	250 mL
1 cup	whipping (35%) cream	250 mL
1 tsp	vanilla	5 mL

1. Spread pine nuts evenly on baking sheet and bake in preheated oven for 3 to 5 minutes or until golden brown. Watch carefully; they burn very quickly. Reserve a handful for topping.

2. In a food processor, purée hot nuts, eggs, honey, sugar and salt until smooth. Transfer to a bowl and set aside.

3. In a medium saucepan over medium-low heat, bring milk to a simmer. Gradually whisk into the egg mixture.

4. Return entire mixture to the saucepan. Cook over low heat, stirring constantly, until the mixture is thick enough to coat the back of a wooden spoon. Be careful not to let it boil. Transfer to a clean large bowl. Let cool to room temperature. Cover and refrigerate until completely cold or overnight.

5. Stir cream mixture. Transfer to an ice cream maker and freeze according to manufacturer's instructions.

6. When serving, top with reserved pine nuts.

Pistachio Ice Cream

SERVES 6

Use unsalted, preferably peeled, raw pistachios for this beautiful pale green ice cream. For a savory finish, dust the top of each serving with crushed salted pistachios. Though this ice cream is very green, if you want it neon, you can add a drop of green food coloring.

Tip: This ice cream will be soft. For firmer ice cream, place in the freezer for at least 2 hours.

1 1/2 cups	shelled unsalted raw pistachios, divided	375 mL
1/2 cup	corn syrup	125 mL
1/2 cup	half-and-half (10%) cream	125 mL
1 cup	table (18%) cream	250 mL
1/4 cup	granulated sugar	50 mL
1 cup	whipping (35%) cream	250 mL
3/4 tsp	vanilla	4 mL
1/4 tsp	salt	1 mL
1/4 tsp	almond extract	1 mL

1. In a food processor or blender, purée 1 cup (250 mL) pistachios, corn syrup and half-and-half until smooth.

2. In a medium saucepan over medium-low heat, bring table cream to a simmer. Add sugar and stir until sugar is dissolved.

3. With the food processor running, gradually pour cream mixture into pistachio mixture. Purée until smooth.

4. Strain into a clean large bowl. Stir in whipping cream, vanilla, salt and almond extract. Cover and refrigerate until completely cold or overnight.

5. Stir cream mixture. Transfer to an ice cream maker and freeze according to manufacturer's instructions. Add remaining pistachios in the last 5 minutes of freezing.

✿ Variation

Turkish Delight Pistachio Ice Cream: Substitute 1 tbsp (15 mL) rose water for the almond extract. Top each serving with a sprinkle of chopped Turkish delight candies.

Kulfi

SERVES 6

There are many variations of this sticky ice cream that is popular in Indian cultures; some even call for the addition of white bread as a thickening agent. Ours is adapted from a recipe by our friend Rosemarie DeSouza, who says that it's tried-and-true and enjoyed by her family members both here and in Goa. Unlike traditional North American ice cream, this one is made using the freezer method and not a machine.

- Kulfi molds, muffin tin or 8-inch (2 L) square baking pan or dish, lined with plastic wrap

1	can (10 oz/300 mL) sweetened condensed partly skimmed milk	1
1	can (14 oz/385 mL) evaporated skim milk	1
1 cup	light (5%) cream	250 mL
2 tsp	ground cardamom	10 mL
1 tsp	vanilla	5 mL
1 cup	pistachios, chopped or whole	250 mL

1. In a large bowl, stir together condensed milk, evaporated milk and cream. Stir in cardamom and vanilla.

2. Pour into kulfi molds, muffin tins or prepared baking pan. Cover with plastic wrap.

3. Freeze for at least 6 hours or overnight. Turn out of molds or muffins cups onto serving plates or scoop out of the square pan or cut into cubes. Serve sprinkled with pistachios.

Maple Walnut Ice Cream

This delicious ice cream owes its unique flavor to toasted walnuts and pure maple syrup. Despite the hundreds of fancy ice cream combinations now available, maple walnut is still a top seller.

Tip: Don't cook your egg mixture over too high a heat or the eggs will scramble. If they do scramble, strain the mixture through a fine sieve.

Serving suggestion: For brunch, serve a scoop of Maple Walnut Ice Cream on toasted waffles with a side of bacon and sliced fresh oranges.

4	egg yolks	4
2/3 cup	pure maple syrup	150 mL
1 tsp	all-purpose flour	5 mL
1/4 tsp	salt	1 mL
1 cup	table (18%) cream	250 mL
1 cup	milk	250 mL
1/2 tsp	vanilla	2 mL
1/2 cup	chopped toasted walnuts (see Tip, page 110)	125 mL

1. In a bowl, whisk together egg yolks, maple syrup, flour and salt until combined. Set aside.

2. In a medium saucepan over medium-low heat, bring cream and milk to a simmer. Gradually whisk into the egg mixture.

3. Return entire mixture to the saucepan. Cook over low heat, stirring constantly, until the mixture is thick enough to coat the back of a wooden spoon. Be careful not to let it boil. Strain into a clean large bowl. Cool to room temperature.

4. Stir in vanilla. Cover and refrigerate until completely cold or overnight.

5. Transfer to an ice cream maker and freeze according to manufacturer's instructions. Add walnuts in the last 5 minutes of freezing and let machine stir them in.

Variation

Caramelized Maple Walnut Ice Cream: Instead of toasting the walnuts, you can caramelize them. In a skillet over medium-high heat, melt 2 tbsp (25 mL) unsalted butter. Sauté walnuts until golden. Add 2 tbsp (25 mL) packed brown sugar. Cook, stirring, until golden brown and nuts are well coated. Let cool completely. Add to ice cream in the last 5 minutes of freezing.

Date and Walnut Ice Cream

Dates get a bad rap, but when mixed with crunchy walnuts, milk and cream, they create a dessert-worthy ice cream!

2	egg yolks	2
1 cup	granulated sugar	250 mL
2 cups	milk	500 mL
2 cups	whipping (35%) cream	500 mL
1 cup	chopped dates	250 mL
1 tbsp	vanilla	15 mL
½ cup	chopped walnuts	125 mL

1. In a bowl, whisk egg yolks with sugar until thickened and pale yellow. Set aside.

2. In a medium saucepan over medium-low heat, bring milk to a simmer. Gradually whisk into the egg mixture.

3. Return entire mixture to the saucepan. Cook over low heat, stirring constantly, until the mixture is thick enough to coat the back of a wooden spoon. Be careful not to let it boil. Strain into a clean large bowl. Let cool to room temperature.

4. Stir in whipping cream, dates and vanilla. Cover and refrigerate until completely cold or overnight.

5. Stir cream mixture. Transfer to an ice cream maker and freeze according to manufacturer's instructions. Add walnuts in the last 5 minutes of freezing and let machine stir them in.

Toasted Sesame and Honey Ice Cream

The flavor of this ice cream is reminiscent of candy sesame snaps, those thin sesame and honey cookies (sometimes referred to as benne wafers) found in gourmet or Middle Eastern grocers.

Tip: If you love sesame seeds, crumble a few sesame snaps (benne wafers) into the ice cream in its final mixing stage.

2	egg yolks	2
1/2 cup	granulated sugar	125 mL
1/2 cup	liquid honey	125 mL
1 1/2 cups	milk	375 mL
1 1/2 cups	whipping (35%) cream	375 mL
1/4 cup	sesame seeds, toasted until golden	50 mL

1. In a bowl, whisk egg yolks with sugar and honey until thickened and pale yellow. Set aside.

2. In a medium saucepan over medium-low heat, bring milk and cream to a simmer. Gradually whisk into the egg mixture.

3. Return entire mixture to the saucepan. Cook over low heat, stirring constantly, until the mixture is thick enough to coat the back of a wooden spoon. Be careful not to let it boil. Strain into a clean large bowl. Let cool to room temperature.

4. Stir in sesame seeds. Cover and refrigerate until completely cold or overnight.

5. Stir cream mixture. Transfer to an ice cream maker and freeze according to manufacturer's instructions.

Beverage-Inspired Ice Creams

Café au Lait Ice Cream

Nothing beats warm milk infused with coffee — nothing except the ice cream version of the popular drink. This buzz-a-licious dessert is so addictive that we've caught people eating it right out of the container in the middle of the night.

Serving suggestion:
For a trendy refresher, make this coffee frosty by placing two scoops of Café au Lait Ice Cream in a beer mug. Top with freshly brewed strong coffee. Garnish with a cinnamon stick.

8	egg yolks	8
1 ½ cups	packed brown sugar	375 mL
4 cups	milk	1 L
2 cups	whipping (35%) cream	500 mL
1 cup	freshly brewed strong coffee	250 mL

1. In a bowl, whisk egg yolks with brown sugar until thickened and pale yellow. Set aside.

2. In a medium saucepan over medium-low heat, bring milk and whipping cream to a simmer. Gradually whisk into the egg mixture.

3. Return entire mixture to the saucepan. Cook over low heat, stirring constantly, until the mixture is thick enough to coat the back of a wooden spoon. Be careful not to let it boil. Strain into a clean large bowl. Let cool to room temperature.

4. Stir in coffee. Cover and refrigerate until completely cold or overnight.

5. Stir cream mixture. Transfer to an ice cream maker and freeze according to manufacturer's instructions.

Variation
Chocolate Coffee Ice Cream: Stir in 6 oz (175 g) bittersweet chocolate, melted, just before the mixture goes into the ice cream maker.

Café Mocha Ice Cream

We make this with espresso beans, but any dark roast will make just as delicious a dessert. For extra-strong flavor, place the beans in a plastic bag, seal the bag and lightly crush them with a rolling pin before adding them to the heated cream to steep.

Tip: Melting chocolate is very easy but requires close attention because it can burn quickly. Our method is to melt it in the top half of a double boiler over simmering water. If you don't have a double boiler, use a saucepan and a stainless-steel bowl. Pour in enough water to come 1 inch (2.5 cm) up side of saucepan. Bring to a simmer over medium heat. Place chocolate in bowl. Place over pan and stir until melted.

2 cups	whipping (35%) cream	500 mL
1 cup	espresso or dark-roasted coffee beans	250 mL
1 cup	milk	250 mL
6	egg yolks	6
½ cup	granulated sugar	125 mL
4 oz	bittersweet chocolate, melted (see Tip, left)	125 g
1 tbsp	coffee-flavored liqueur (optional)	15 mL

1. In a medium saucepan over medium-low heat, bring cream, espresso beans and milk just to a boil. Remove from heat and let stand for 1 hour. Strain into a bowl and set aside.

2. In a separate bowl, whisk egg yolks with sugar until thickened and pale yellow. Set aside.

3. Return cream mixture to the saucepan. Bring to a simmer over medium-low heat. Gradually whisk into the egg mixture.

4. Return entire mixture to the saucepan. Cook over low heat, stirring constantly, until the mixture is thick enough to coat the back of a wooden spoon. Be careful not to let it boil. Strain into a clean large bowl. Let cool to room temperature.

5. Stir in melted chocolate. Cover and refrigerate until completely cold or overnight.

6. Stir cream mixture. Transfer to an ice cream maker and freeze according to manufacturer's instructions. Add coffee-flavored liqueur, if using, in the last 5 minutes of freezing and let machine stir it in.

❧ Variation

Chocolate Espresso Bean Ice Cream: Add ½ cup (125 mL) chocolate-covered espresso beans in the last 5 minutes of freezing and let machine stir them in.

Espresso Chocolate Chip Ice Cream

SERVES 4 TO 6

We don't scrimp on the coffee flavor, but you can add less — or even a bit more — espresso powder, depending on how much you need a caffeine hit.

5	egg yolks	5
⅔ cup	granulated sugar	150 mL
2 cups	milk	500 mL
½ cup	whipping (35%) cream	125 mL
1 tsp	vanilla	5 mL
1 cup	semisweet chocolate chips	250 mL
2 tbsp	instant espresso powder	25 mL

1. In a bowl, whisk egg yolks with sugar until thickened and pale yellow. Set aside.

2. In a medium saucepan over medium-low heat, bring milk and cream to a simmer. Gradually whisk into the egg mixture.

3. Return entire mixture to the saucepan. Cook over low heat, stirring constantly, until the mixture is thick enough to coat the back of a wooden spoon. Be careful not to let it boil. Strain into a clean large bowl. Let cool to room temperature.

4. Stir in vanilla. Cover and refrigerate until completely cold or overnight.

5. Stir cream mixture. Transfer to an ice cream maker and freeze according to manufacturer's instructions. Add chocolate chips and espresso powder in the last 5 minutes of freezing and let machine stir them in.

❧ Variation

A quick version of this dessert can be made with store-bought vanilla ice cream: Refrigerate a 1-pint (500 mL) container of your favorite vanilla ice cream until it is smooth enough to mix in the espresso powder and chocolate chips. Mix well, spoon back into the container and freeze.

Green Tea Ice Cream

With Asian menus so popular these days, this dessert has begun to pop up everywhere. It's a terrific ending after sushi or stir-fries.

2 cups	milk	500 mL
1 cup	whipping (35%) cream	250 mL
3 tbsp	green tea leaves or green tea with mint	45 mL
2	egg yolks	2
¾ cup	granulated sugar	175 mL
1 tbsp	cornstarch	15 mL

1. In a medium saucepan over medium-low heat, bring milk and cream to a simmer. Remove from heat. Stir in green tea leaves and let stand for 10 minutes.

2. In a bowl, whisk egg yolks with sugar until thickened and pale yellow. Whisk in cornstarch. Gradually whisk in cream mixture.

3. Return entire mixture to the saucepan. Cook over low heat, stirring constantly, until the mixture is thick enough to coat the back of a wooden spoon. Be careful not to let it boil. Strain into a clean large bowl. Let cool to room temperature. Cover and refrigerate until completely cold or overnight.

4. Stir cream mixture. Transfer to an ice cream maker and freeze according to manufacturer's instructions.

Masala Chai Ice Cream

- Mortar and pestle

½	cinnamon stick	½
8	black peppercorns	8
6	whole cloves	6
3	cardamom pods	3
2 cups	water	500 mL
3	slices gingerroot (each ¼ inch/0.5 cm thick)	3
½ cup	milk	125 mL
1 cup	Simple Syrup (see recipe, page 20)	250 mL
½ cup	whipping (35%) cream	125 mL

1. Using a mortar and pestle, crush cinnamon, peppercorns, cloves and cardamom until fine and powdery (see Tip, left).

2. In a medium saucepan over medium-high heat, bring peppercorn mixture, water, ginger and milk to a boil. Remove from heat. Cover and let stand for 10 minutes. Strain into a clean large bowl. Let cool to room temperature.

3. Stir in syrup and cream. Cover and refrigerate until completely cold or overnight.

4. Stir cream mixture. Transfer to an ice cream maker and freeze according to manufacturer's instructions.

Eggnog Ice Cream

SERVES 8 TO 10

This perfect ice cream for the holidays can be made with store-bought eggnog, as in the Variation (below), or by following this traditional recipe for an egg-custard base. It can be tricky to find a carton of store-bought eggnog in July, but this recipe means you can make this treat all year round.

Tip: We used 2 tbsp (25 mL) rum extract because we like flavors exaggerated. If you don't prefer such a strong rum flavor, feel free to reduce the extract to 1 tbsp (15 mL).

Do not use too much alcohol; if you do, you'll have a hard time getting your ice cream to freeze.

8	egg yolks	8
1 1/4 cups	granulated sugar	300 mL
3 cups	milk	750 mL
1 cup	whipping (35%) cream	250 mL
2 tbsp	rum extract or rum (see Tips, left)	25 mL
1 tbsp	vanilla	15 mL
1 tsp	brandy	5 mL
1/4 tsp	ground nutmeg	1 mL
1/4 tsp	ground cinnamon	1 mL

1. In a bowl, whisk egg yolks with sugar until thickened and pale yellow. Set aside.

2. In a medium saucepan over medium-low heat, bring milk and cream to a simmer. Gradually whisk into the egg mixture.

3. Return entire mixture to the saucepan. Cook over low heat, stirring constantly, until the mixture is thick enough to coat the back of a wooden spoon. Be careful not to let it boil. Strain into a clean large bowl. Let cool to room temperature.

4. Stir in rum extract, vanilla, brandy, nutmeg and cinnamon until thoroughly blended. Cover and refrigerate until completely cold or overnight.

5. Stir cream mixture. Transfer to an ice cream maker and freeze according to manufacturer's instructions.

Variation

Quick Eggnog Ice Cream: To make ice cream from store-bought eggnog, omit egg yolks, sugar, milk, cream and vanilla. In a bowl, stir together 4 cups (1 L) store-bought eggnog, rum extract, brandy, nutmeg and cinnamon. Transfer to an ice cream maker and freeze according to manufacturer's instructions.

Cola Ice Cream

This is a favorite recipe of preteens, who enjoy the slushy, syrupy texture and love to experiment with different soda pops. Our favorites, though, are traditional cola and root beer.

Tip: We have used 2% milk here and in several other recipes. Not only does it reduce the fat content, but it tastes just as good as whole milk. If you prefer a full-fat version, use whole milk instead.

1	can (12 oz/325 mL) soda pop, preferably cola or root beer	1
2 cups	2% milk (see Tip, left)	500 mL
1 cup	half-and-half (10%) cream	250 mL
¼ cup	granulated sugar	50 mL

1. In a bowl, stir together pop, milk, cream and sugar.

2. Transfer to an ice cream maker and freeze according to manufacturer's instructions.

❧ Variations

Cherry Cola Ice Cream: Add 1 tbsp (15 mL) cherry syrup.

Vanilla Cola Ice Cream: Add ½ tsp (2 mL) vanilla.

Guinness Ice Cream

This has the slight bitterness of a good pint of stout and is absolutely delicious with a fruit crumble or Irish soda bread pudding. It provides good conversation value as well as taste.

Tip: This ice cream will be soft. For firmer ice cream, place in the freezer for at least 2 hours.

2	egg yolks	2
¾ cup	granulated sugar	175 mL
3 cups	Guinness Draught, about 1 ½ cans	750 mL
½ cup	milk	125 mL
1 cup	whipping (35%) cream	250 mL

1. In a bowl, whisk egg yolks with sugar until thickened and pale yellow. Set aside.

2. In a medium saucepan over medium heat, cook Guinness, stirring occasionally, until reduced by half. Reduce heat to low. Stir in milk. Bring to a simmer. Gradually whisk into the egg mixture.

3. Return entire mixture to the saucepan. Cook over low heat, stirring constantly, until the mixture is thick enough to coat the back of a wooden spoon. Be careful not to let it boil. Strain into a clean large bowl. Let cool to room temperature.

4. Stir in whipping cream. Cover and refrigerate until completely cold or overnight.

5. Stir cream mixture. Transfer to an ice cream maker and freeze according to manufacturer's instructions.

Champagne Ice Cream

If you are looking for an elegant ice cream to serve at a celebratory dinner party, this is definitely the one!

Tip: For a special garnish, top with puréed or chopped fresh fruit.

2	egg yolks	2
1 cup	granulated sugar	250 mL
½ cup	corn syrup	125 mL
2 cups	milk	500 mL
2 cups	whipping (35%) cream	500 mL
¾ cup	Champagne or other sparkling wine	175 mL
1 tbsp	vanilla	15 mL

1. In a bowl, whisk egg yolks with sugar and corn syrup until thickened and pale yellow. Set aside.

2. In a medium saucepan over medium-low heat, bring milk to a simmer. Gradually whisk into the egg mixture.

3. Return entire mixture to the saucepan. Cook over low heat, stirring constantly, until the mixture is thick enough to coat the back of a wooden spoon. Be careful not to let it boil. Strain into a clean large bowl. Let cool to room temperature.

4. Stir in whipping cream, Champagne and vanilla. Cover and refrigerate until completely cold or overnight.

5. Stir cream mixture. Transfer to an ice cream maker and freeze according to manufacturer's instructions.

Sweet & Savory Ice Creams

Carrot Ginger Ice Cream

It works as a soup, so why not an ice cream? It tastes just like sweet carrot juice. It may sound odd, but it's delicious. Just try it.

2	egg yolks	2
1 cup	granulated sugar	250 mL
2 cups	milk	500 mL
1 cup	whipping (35%) cream	250 mL
2 cups	carrot juice	500 mL
3 tbsp	grated gingerroot	45 mL

1. In a bowl, whisk egg yolks with sugar until thickened and pale yellow. Set aside.

2. In a medium saucepan over medium-low heat, bring milk to a simmer. Gradually whisk into the egg mixture.

3. Return entire mixture to the saucepan. Cook over low heat, stirring constantly, until the mixture is thick enough to coat the back of a wooden spoon. Be careful not to let it boil. Strain into a clean large bowl. Let cool to room temperature.

4. Stir in whipping cream, carrot juice and ginger. Cover and refrigerate until completely cold or overnight.

5. Stir cream mixture. Transfer to an ice cream maker and freeze according to manufacturer's instructions.

Corn Ice Cream

Skeptics are transformed into fans when they try this absolutely delicious treat. This unusual ice cream, with the hint of maple syrup, is a terrific topping for cornbread, gingerbread or lemon pound cake. If you prefer a smoother texture, pass the corn through a food mill before adding it to the cream mixture.

Tip: Do not substitute fresh corn for the cream-style corn, which works best in this recipe.

3	egg yolks	3
½ cup	granulated sugar	125 mL
¾ cup	pure maple syrup	175 mL
1 cup	half-and-half (10%) cream	250 mL
1 cup	whipping (35%) cream	250 mL
1	can (14 oz/398 mL) cream-style corn (see Tip, left)	1
1 tsp	vanilla	5 mL

1. In a bowl, whisk egg yolks with sugar until thickened and pale yellow. Whisk in maple syrup. Set aside.

2. In a medium saucepan over medium-low heat, bring half-and-half and whipping cream to a simmer. Gradually whisk into the egg mixture.

3. Return entire mixture to the saucepan. Cook over low heat, stirring constantly, until the mixture is thick enough to coat the back of a wooden spoon. Be careful not to let it boil. Strain into a clean large bowl. Let cool to room temperature.

4. Stir in corn and vanilla. Cover and refrigerate until completely cold or overnight.

5. Stir cream mixture. Transfer to an ice cream maker and freeze according to manufacturer's instructions.

Roasted Garlic Ice Cream

SERVES 4 TO 6

Roasting garlic mellows its flavor and gives it a bit of a nuttiness. But make no mistake: this ice cream is for garlic lovers only. Some recipes call for 5 heads of garlic, which, to us, sounds like a bit of overkill.

Tip: We have used 2% milk here and in several other recipes. Not only does it reduce the fat content, but it tastes just as good as whole milk. If you prefer a full-fat version, use whole milk instead.

• Preheat oven to 350°F (180°C)

2	heads garlic	2
2 tsp	olive oil	10 mL
3	egg yolks	3
1/4 cup	granulated sugar	50 mL
1 cup	table (18%) cream	250 mL
1/2 cup	2% milk (see Tip, left)	125 mL
1 cup	whipping (35%) cream	250 mL
1/8 tsp	salt	0.5 mL

1. Cut 1/4 inch (0.5 cm) off tops of garlic heads. Place each head on a large square of foil. Drizzle with oil. Pull up foil around garlic and seal to make two packages. Roast in preheated oven for 30 minutes.

2. Open foil to expose garlic. Return to oven and roast for another 30 minutes or until soft and browned. Remove from oven. When cool enough to handle, squeeze garlic out into bowl. Set aside.

3. In a separate bowl, whisk egg yolks with sugar until thickened and pale yellow. Set aside.

4. In a medium saucepan over medium-low heat, bring table cream, milk and half of the roasted garlic to a simmer. Reduce heat to low. Simmer, stirring often, for 15 minutes or until thickened. Gradually whisk into the egg mixture.

Tip: This ice cream will be soft. For firmer ice cream, place in the freezer for at least 2 hours.

5. Return entire mixture to the saucepan. Cook over low heat, stirring constantly, until the mixture is thick enough to coat the back of a wooden spoon. Be careful not to let it boil. Strain into a clean large bowl. Let cool to room temperature.

6. Stir in whipping cream and salt. Cover and refrigerate until completely cold or overnight.

7. Stir the cream mixture. Transfer to an ice cream maker and freeze according to manufacturer's instructions. Add remaining roasted garlic in the last 5 minutes of freezing and let machine stir it in.

Pumpkin Ice Cream

If you can't wait until Thanksgiving for the taste of pumpkin pie, try making this ice cream instead. Don't bother using fresh pumpkin — the canned variety is silky smooth and the key to this recipe's success.

Tip: Make sure you buy 100% pumpkin purée, not a blend of pumpkin and other squashes.

Serving suggestion: For a frozen pumpkin pie, spoon softened Pumpkin Ice Cream into a 9-inch (23 cm) store-bought graham cracker crust. Freeze until firm. To serve, top with whipped cream rosettes and chocolate shavings.

4	egg yolks	4
¾ cup	granulated sugar	175 mL
2 cups	whipping (35%) cream	500 mL
2 cups	milk	500 mL
1 cup	unsweetened pumpkin purée (not pie filling)	250 mL
1 tsp	ground cinnamon	5 mL
1 tsp	ground nutmeg	5 mL
1 tsp	ground ginger	5 mL
1 tsp	vanilla	5 mL

1. In a bowl, whisk egg yolks with sugar until thickened and pale yellow. Set aside.

2. In a medium saucepan over medium-low heat, bring cream and milk to a simmer. Gradually whisk into the egg mixture.

3. Return entire mixture to the saucepan. Cook over low heat, stirring constantly, until the mixture is thick enough to coat the back of a wooden spoon. Be careful not to let it boil. Strain into a clean large bowl. Let cool to room temperature.

4. Whisk in pumpkin purée, in two additions, until smooth. Stir in cinnamon, nutmeg, ginger and vanilla. Cover and refrigerate until completely cold or overnight.

5. Stir cream mixture. Transfer to an ice cream maker and freeze according to manufacturer's instructions.

Brown Bread Ice Cream

SERVES 6

Though unusual, this ice cream is one of the best we've ever had. Because the bread crumbs are caramelized, the result is more like pralines than bread pudding.

Tips: We have used 2% milk here and in several other recipes. Not only does it reduce the fat content, but it tastes just as good as whole milk. If you prefer a full-fat version, use whole milk instead.

The success of this ice cream depends on the whole wheat bread. Don't substitute white bread for it.

Serving suggestion: Like your favorite bread pudding, this ice cream is amazing drizzled with buttery Sticky Sauce (see recipe, page 255).

4	egg yolks	4
1/3 cup	granulated sugar	75 mL
1 1/2 cups	2% milk (see Tips, left)	375 mL
1 cup	whipping (35%) cream	250 mL
1 tsp	lemon zest	5 mL
1 tsp	vanilla	5 mL
3 tbsp	unsalted butter	45 mL
1 1/2 cups	fresh whole wheat bread crumbs	375 mL
1/2 cup	packed brown sugar	125 mL

1. In a bowl, whisk egg yolks with granulated sugar until thickened and pale yellow. Set aside.

2. In a medium saucepan over medium-low heat, bring milk to a simmer. Gradually whisk into the egg mixture.

3. Return entire mixture to the saucepan. Cook over low heat, stirring constantly, until the mixture is thick enough to coat the back of a wooden spoon. Be careful not to let it boil. Strain into a clean large bowl. Let cool to room temperature.

4. Stir in whipping cream, lemon zest and vanilla. Cover and refrigerate until completely cold or overnight.

5. Meanwhile, in another medium saucepan over medium heat, melt butter. Add bread crumbs and brown sugar. Cook, stirring, for 4 to 5 minutes or until golden brown and bread crumbs are evenly coated. Drain on paper towel–lined plate.

6. Stir cream mixture. Transfer to an ice cream maker and freeze according to manufacturer's instructions. Add bread crumb mixture in the last 5 minutes of freezing and let machine stir it in.

Oatmeal Ice Cream

Who would have thought that an ordinary breakfast cereal could make such a wonderful frozen dessert? Serving ideas are endless for this perfect brunch treat, including sliced bananas, pancakes or fresh berries. Or scoop out half a cantaloupe and fill with a scoop of Oatmeal Ice Cream, then sprinkle with granola. For dessert, serve a scoop on Baked Apples (see recipe, opposite). Use old-fashioned rolled oats, not instant oatmeal or quick-cooking rolled oats.

Tip: This ice cream will be soft. For firmer ice cream, place in the freezer for at least 2 hours.

3	egg yolks	3
3/4 cup	granulated sugar	175 mL
1 cup	2% milk (see Tip, page 137)	250 mL
1 cup	half-and-half (10%) cream	250 mL
1/2 cup	old-fashioned rolled oats	125 mL
1/2 tsp	salt	2 mL
1/2 tsp	ground cinnamon	2 mL
1 1/2 cups	whipping (35%) cream	375 mL
1/2 cup	pure maple syrup	125 mL

1. In a bowl, whisk egg yolks with sugar until thickened and pale yellow. Set aside.

2. In a medium saucepan over medium heat, bring milk and half-and-half to a simmer. Add oats, salt and cinnamon. Cook, stirring constantly, for 10 minutes or until thick and creamy. Gradually whisk into the egg mixture.

3. Let cool for 15 minutes. Stir in whipping cream and maple syrup. Cover and refrigerate until completely cold or overnight.

4. Stir cream mixture. Transfer to an ice cream maker and freeze according to manufacturer's instructions.

Baked Apples

For a great comfort-food dessert, serve these baked apples warm
with a scoop of Oatmeal Ice Cream (see recipe, opposite)
and drizzle with pure maple syrup.

- **Preheat oven to 375°F (190°C)**
- **8-inch (2 L) square glass baking dish**

6	medium cooking apples	6
1 cup	packed brown sugar	250 mL
1/2 cup	golden raisins	125 mL
1/4 cup	unsalted butter, cut into cubes	50 mL
1/4 cup	water	50 mL

1. Using a potato peeler, peel the top one-third of each apple. Core, leaving bottoms intact.

2. Cut horizontally through the skin around the middle of each apple to prevent it from splitting as it cooks.

3. In a small bowl, combine brown sugar, raisins and butter until crumbly. Dividing mixture evenly among apples, spoon into cavities.

4. Place stuffed apples in baking dish. Sprinkle water in the pan. Bake in preheated oven for 30 minutes or until apples are soft and topping is bubbly.

 SERVES 6

Rice Pudding Ice Cream

SERVES 4 TO 6

We adore rice pudding and decided to turn this comfort food into ice cream. But instead of long-grain rice, we used the short-grain Arborio we rely on for risotto. Sometimes we add 1 cup (250 mL) golden raisins to the mix. Often we add 1 tbsp (15 mL) lemon or orange zest. This recipe is rather exotic, with its licorice anise taste. You can substitute cinnamon in place of the aniseed for a more traditional flavor. It's a great dessert to complement an Indian dinner — especially if you replace the aniseed with cardamom.

Tip: This ice cream will be soft. For firmer ice cream, place in the freezer for at least 2 hours.

You'll need about ½ cup (125 mL) raw rice to make 1 cup (250 mL) cooked.

1 cup	cooked Arborio or other short-grain rice (see Tips, left)	250 mL
1 cup	milk	250 mL
1 cup	table (18%) cream	250 mL
¾ cup	granulated sugar	175 mL
2	eggs	2
½ cup	whipping (35%) cream	125 mL
1 tsp	ground aniseed	5 mL
¼ tsp	vanilla	1 mL

1. In a medium saucepan over medium heat, bring rice, milk, table cream and sugar to a simmer. Cook, stirring occasionally, until sugar is dissolved. Reduce heat to low. Simmer, stirring occasionally, for 30 minutes or until thick and creamy. Stir constantly in the last 5 minutes to prevent sticking. Be careful not to let it boil. Let cool to room temperature.

2. In a large bowl, whisk eggs until pale yellow. Gradually whisk in rice mixture.

3. Stir in whipping cream, aniseed and vanilla. Cover and refrigerate until completely cold or overnight.

4. Stir cream mixture. Transfer to an ice cream maker and freeze according to manufacturer's instructions.

Instant Rice Pudding Ice Cream

2	cans (each 15 oz/425 mL) rice pudding	2
1 cup	Simple Syrup (see recipe, page 20)	250 mL
½ tsp	vanilla	2 mL
	Zest of 1 lemon	

1. In a bowl, stir together rice pudding, syrup, vanilla and lemon zest.

2. Transfer to an ice cream maker and freeze according to manufacturer's instructions.

> **Variation**
> *Cinnamon-Spiced Instant Rice Pudding Ice Cream:* Add 1 tsp (5 mL) cinnamon and ¼ tsp (1 mL) ground nutmeg to rice pudding mixture before freezing.

Red Bean Ice Cream

SERVES 8

Asian markets abound in major urban centers. That's where you'll find sweetened red bean paste, a mainstay of Chinese pastries and the ingredient that transforms an ordinary chilled custard into an exotic frozen treat.

2	egg yolks	2
½ cup	granulated sugar	125 mL
1 cup	whipping (35%) cream	250 mL
1 cup	milk	250 mL
1¼ cups	sweetened red bean paste	300 mL

1. In a bowl, whisk egg yolks with sugar until thickened and pale yellow. Set aside.

2. In a medium saucepan over medium-low heat, bring cream and milk to a simmer. Gradually whisk into the egg mixture.

3. Return entire mixture to the saucepan. Cook over low heat, stirring constantly, until the mixture is thick enough to coat the back of a wooden spoon. Be careful not to let it boil. Strain into a clean large bowl. Let cool to room temperature.

4. Whisk in red bean paste. Cover and refrigerate until completely cold or overnight.

5. Stir cream mixture. Transfer to an ice cream maker and freeze according to manufacturer's instructions.

Variation
Add ¼ cup (50 mL) finely chopped crystallized ginger in the last 5 minutes of freezing and let machine stir it in.

Tahini Ice Cream

SERVES 8

You won't believe how good this ice cream is. It's creamy in texture, with the nutty taste of sesame seeds! Forget about vanilla — try this with your next wedge of apple pie!

2 cups	whipping (35%) cream	500 mL
2 cups	milk	500 mL
1 cup	granulated sugar	250 mL
1 cup	tahini	250 mL
1 tsp	vanilla	5 mL
Pinch	salt	Pinch

1. In a large bowl, whisk together cream, milk, sugar, tahini, vanilla and salt. Cover and refrigerate until completely cold or overnight.

2. Stir cream mixture. Transfer to an ice cream maker and freeze according to manufacturer's instructions.

Tahini Basics

Tahini is a creamy paste made from ground sesame seeds. It is used extensively throughout Middle Eastern cuisine — in desserts, in dressings and often in the popular appetizer dip hummus.

Parmesan Ice Cream

Serve this savory ice cream with crisp pears as an interesting part of your cheese course. Or try topping it with pesto and roasted tomatoes for an ice cream take on the classic Pizza Margarita.

Tip: When the cream and Parmesan mixture cools, it becomes too thick for ice cream makers with prefrozen canisters. If you have an ice cream maker with a built-in compressor, you'll have no problem.

3 cups	table (18%) cream	750 mL
2 cups	freshly grated Parmesan cheese	500 mL
Pinch	freshly ground white pepper	Pinch
	Salt	

1. In a medium saucepan over medium-low heat, bring cream to a simmer. Gradually whisk in Parmesan cheese until completely melted. Add pepper and salt to taste. Strain into a clean bowl.

2. *Option 1:* If using an ice cream maker with built-in compressor (see Tip, left), follow manufacturer's instructions.

3. *Option 2:* Place the bowl full of ice cream mixture inside a bigger bowl full of ice. Whisk the mixture until it becomes thick. Scrape into a small loaf pan, cover and place in freezer. When ready to enjoy, warm pan in hot water, invert onto a cutting board and cut slices from the ice cream loaf, or use a scoop.

Mango Ice Cream Brûlée (page 92)

Pine Nut and Honey Ice Cream (page 115)

Green Tea Ice Cream (page 125)

Tomato Basil Ice (page 228)

Blueberry Ginger Ice (page 184)

Pumpkin Ice Cream (page 136)

Peppermint Chocolate Chip
Ice Cream (page 150)

Coffee Almond Brownie
Ice Cream (page 151)

Kids' Favorite Ice Creams

Kids' Cooler

SERVES 2

On a hot summer day, kids will welcome this ice cream craft. It won't result in premium-quality ice cream, but it's a fun idea and it beautifully demonstrates the old-fashioned ice-and-salt method of making ice cream.

- 1 sandwich-size resealable plastic bag
- 1 large-size resealable plastic freezer bag

¾ cup	half-and-half (10%) cream	175 mL
1 tbsp	granulated sugar	15 mL
1 tbsp	chocolate syrup	15 mL
½ tsp	vanilla	2 mL
	Ice cubes	
6 tbsp	rock salt	90 mL

1. In the sandwich-size bag, combine cream, sugar, chocolate syrup and vanilla. Seal bag.

2. Fill large-size plastic bag halfway with ice cubes. Add rock salt, then sandwich-size bag. Seal bag.

3. Shake bags vigorously for 8 to 10 minutes or until thickened and mixture turns into ice cream.

Peanut Butter and Banana Ice Cream

If Elvis were around today, he'd be "All Shook Up" by this ice cream. The combination of smashed, mushy bananas and peanut butter is to die for and is definitely a kid-pleaser. For a more decadent ice cream, add the chocolate chips.

2	eggs	2
1 cup	granulated sugar	250 mL
2 cups	milk	500 mL
3	ripe bananas, mashed (1¼ cups/300 mL)	3
2 cups	whipping (35%) cream	500 mL
1 cup	creamy peanut butter	250 mL
½ cup	semisweet chocolate chips (optional)	125 mL

1. In a bowl, whisk eggs with sugar until thickened and pale yellow. Set aside.

2. In a medium saucepan over medium-low heat, bring milk to a simmer. Gradually whisk into the egg mixture.

3. Return entire mixture to the saucepan. Cook over low heat, stirring constantly, until the mixture is thick enough to coat the back of a wooden spoon. Be careful not to let it boil. Strain into a clean large bowl. Let cool to room temperature.

4. Whisk in bananas, whipping cream and peanut butter. Cover and refrigerate until completely cold or overnight.

5. Stir cream mixture. Transfer to an ice cream maker and freeze according to manufacturer's instructions. Add chocolate chips (if using) in the last 5 minutes of freezing and let machine stir them in.

Peanut Butter Chocolate Ice Cream

SERVES 8 TO 10

For many people, this is the ultimate combination. We leave the decision of whether to use smooth or chunky peanut butter up to you. The better the chocolate, the better this tastes.

Tip: This ice cream will be soft. For firmer ice cream, place in the freezer for at least 2 hours.

3	eggs	3
1 ½ cups	granulated sugar	375 mL
8 oz	bittersweet chocolate, finely chopped	250 g
2 cups	half-and-half (10%) cream	500 mL
1 cup	whipping (35%) cream	250 mL
1 tsp	vanilla	5 mL
¾ cup	peanut butter	175 mL

1. In a bowl, whisk eggs with sugar until thickened and pale yellow. Set aside.

2. In a medium saucepan, combine chocolate and half-and-half. Cook over low heat, stirring occasionally, until chocolate is melted. Gradually whisk into the egg mixture.

3. Return entire mixture to the saucepan. Cook over low heat, stirring constantly, until the mixture is thick enough to coat the back of a wooden spoon. Be careful not to let it boil. Strain into a clean large bowl. Let cool to room temperature.

4. Stir in whipping cream and vanilla. Cover and refrigerate until completely cold or overnight.

5. Stir cream mixture. Transfer 1 cup (250 mL) to a small bowl. Whisk in peanut butter until blended. Stir peanut butter mixture into remaining cream mixture.

6. Transfer to an ice cream maker and freeze according to manufacturer's instructions.

Mars Bar Ice Cream

What would happen if you melted a candy bar into a gooey paste and popped it into the freezer to chill? Well, that's what we wondered. We tried making various chocolate bar ice creams, and this was the hands-down winner. Up the wow factor by topping with chopped-up pieces of the Snickers bar.

1 cup	milk	250 mL
4	Mars bars (each 2 oz/58 g), chopped	4
2 cups	whipping (35%) cream	500 mL
1	Snickers bar (2 oz/58 g), chopped into bite-size pieces and chilled	1

1. In a medium saucepan over medium-low heat, bring milk to a simmer. Be careful not to let it boil. Add Mars bars and stir until completely melted. Remove from heat and let cool to room temperature.

2. Stir in whipping cream. Cover and refrigerate until completely cold or overnight.

3. Stir cream mixture. Transfer to an ice cream maker and freeze according to manufacturer's instructions. When the mixture is thick but not solid, add half the Snickers bar pieces and let machine stir them in.

4. When serving, top with the remaining Snickers bar pieces.

Peppermint Chocolate Chip Ice Cream

SERVES 6

This cool, refreshing ice cream is a hit with both kids and adults. Just ask five-year-old Charley, who gobbles it up whenever it's made. If you're a true fan of this classic combo, you might want to add some green food coloring to make sure it looks minty. This version is white and packs a refreshing punch.

Tip: You can use crème de menthe to make this ice cream green and extra minty. Add only 1 tbsp (15 mL) crème de menthe to the strained cream mixture or the ice cream won't freeze properly.

Serving suggestion: To dress up this dessert, serve scoops in store-bought chocolate cups, available at grocery stores. Garnish with sprigs of fresh mint.

2	egg yolks	2
¾ cup	granulated sugar	175 mL
1 cup	whipping (35%) cream	250 mL
1 cup	table (18%) cream	250 mL
1 cup	milk	250 mL
2 tbsp	peppermint extract	25 mL
½ cup	finely chopped bittersweet chocolate	125 mL

1. In a bowl, whisk egg yolks with sugar until thickened and pale yellow. Set aside.

2. In a medium saucepan over medium-low heat, bring whipping cream, table cream and milk to a simmer. Gradually whisk into the egg mixture.

3. Return entire mixture to the saucepan. Cook over low heat, stirring constantly, until the mixture is thick enough to coat the back of a wooden spoon. Be careful not to let it boil. Strain into a clean large bowl. Let cool to room temperature.

4. Stir in peppermint extract. Cover and refrigerate until completely cold or overnight.

5. Stir cream mixture. Transfer to an ice cream maker and freeze according to manufacturer's instructions. Add chocolate in the last 5 minutes of freezing and let machine stir it in.

Variation

Double Mint Ice Cream: Substitute ½ cup (125 mL) chopped chocolate-covered after-dinner mint wafers for bittersweet chocolate.

Coffee Almond Brownie Ice Cream

SERVES 6 TO 8

*Save this ice cream
for a special family
occasion — it's a hit
with kids of all ages.*

Tip: To turn this into a
festive ice cream cake,
transfer the still-soft ice
cream from the ice cream
maker to a springform
pan lined with plastic
wrap and let it set in the
freezer. Decorate with
fresh raspberries,
whipped cream and
crumbled chocolate
brownies.

2	eggs	2
½ cup	granulated sugar	125 mL
2 cups	whipping (35%) cream	500 mL
1 cup	milk	250 mL
3 tbsp	instant espresso powder	45 mL
½ cup	chopped almonds, toasted	125 mL
1 cup	crumbled chocolate brownies	250 mL

1. In a bowl, whisk eggs with sugar until thickened and pale yellow. Set aside.

2. In a medium saucepan over medium-low heat, bring cream, milk and espresso powder to a simmer. Gradually whisk into the egg mixture.

3. Return entire mixture to the saucepan. Cook over low heat, stirring constantly, until the mixture is thick enough to coat the back of a wooden spoon. Be careful not to let it boil. Strain into a clean large bowl. Let cool to room temperature. Cover and refrigerate until completely cold or overnight.

4. Stir cream mixture. Transfer to an ice cream maker and freeze according to manufacturer's instructions. Add almonds and brownies in the last 5 minutes of freezing and let machine stir them in.

Cookies and Cream Ice Cream

Any cookie you dunk in milk will make a tasty addition to this dessert, which is based on an excellent basic vanilla ice cream.

Tips: This ice cream will be soft. For firmer ice cream, place in the freezer for at least 2 hours.

Remember to add the cookies at the very end of churning or they'll get too soggy.

To simplify the preparation, use 2 tsp (10 mL) vanilla extract instead of steeping the vanilla pod in the milk. Add the vanilla right before refrigerating.

Serving suggestion: For a children's party, scoop balls of ice cream onto parchment paper–lined cookie sheet. Top each with a sugar cone to make a hat and use candy to make faces. Think wizards, witches and clowns.

3	egg yolks	3
6 tbsp	granulated sugar	90 mL
1	vanilla bean (see Tip, left)	1
1 1/2 cups	2% milk (see Tip, page 137)	375 mL
1 1/2 cups	whipping (35%) cream	375 mL
1 1/2 cups	crushed cookies, such as chocolate sandwich cookies	375 mL

1. In a bowl, whisk egg yolks with sugar until thickened and pale yellow. Set aside.

2. Slit vanilla bean lengthwise and scrape seeds into a medium saucepan. Add vanilla pod, milk and cream. Place saucepan over medium-low heat and bring mixture just to a simmer. Remove from heat. Let stand for 15 minutes, allowing the flavor of the vanilla to infuse.

3. Discard pod. Bring mixture to a simmer over medium-low heat and simmer for 5 minutes. Gradually whisk into the egg mixture.

4. Return entire mixture to the saucepan. Cook over low heat, stirring constantly, until the mixture is thick enough to coat the back of a wooden spoon. Be careful not to let it boil. Strain into a clean large bowl. Let cool to room temperature. Cover and refrigerate until completely cold or overnight.

5. Stir cream mixture. Transfer to an ice cream maker and freeze according to manufacturer's instructions.

6. Add cookies in the last 5 minutes of freezing and let machine stir them in.

Variation

Cake and Cream Ice Cream: You can mix in cakes and crumbs, too. For maximum crunchiness, dry them out in a 200°F (100°C) oven for 5 to 10 minutes. Let cool to room temperature. Add in the last 5 minutes of freezing.

Bubble Gum Ice Cream

SERVES 8

This makes a gorgeous pink ice cream that's an all-time kids' favorite. The mini gumballs make it truly authentic, but it's still delicious without them.

3	egg yolks	3
¾ cup	granulated sugar	175 mL
1½ cups	whipping (35%) cream	375 mL
1½ cups	milk	375 mL
4 oz	pink bubble gum (such as Bazooka or Dubble Bubble), chopped into ¼-inch (0.5 cm) pieces	125 g
½ cup	mini gumballs (optional)	125 mL

1. In a bowl, whisk egg yolks with sugar until thickened and pale yellow. Set aside.

2. In a medium saucepan over medium-low heat, bring cream and milk to a simmer. Add chopped bubble gum and remove from heat. Let stand for 15 minutes, stirring occasionally.

3. Using the back of a wooden spoon, press cream mixture through a fine sieve into a bowl to remove any leftover gum pieces. Gradually whisk into the egg mixture.

4. Return entire mixture to the saucepan. Cook over low heat, stirring constantly, until the mixture is thick enough to coat the back of a wooden spoon. Be careful not to let it boil. Strain into a clean large bowl. Let cool to room temperature. Cover and refrigerate until completely cold or overnight.

5. Stir cream mixture. Transfer to an ice cream maker and freeze according to manufacturer's instructions. Add mini gumballs, if using, in the last 5 minutes of freezing and let machine stir them in.

Maraschino Cherry Ice Cream

5	egg yolks	5
2/3 cup	granulated sugar	150 mL
2 cups	milk	500 mL
1/2 cup	whipping (35%) cream	125 mL
1/4 cup	maraschino cherry juice	50 mL
1 tsp	vanilla	5 mL
1/3 cup	finely chopped maraschino cherries	75 mL

1. In a bowl, whisk egg yolks with sugar until thickened and pale yellow. Set aside.

2. In a medium saucepan over medium-low heat, bring milk to a simmer. Gradually whisk into the egg mixture.

3. Return entire mixture to the saucepan. Cook over low heat, stirring constantly, until the mixture is thick enough to coat the back of a wooden spoon. Be careful not to let it boil. Strain into a clean large bowl. Let cool to room temperature.

4. Stir in whipping cream, cherry juice and vanilla. Cover and refrigerate until completely cold or overnight.

5. Stir cream mixture. Transfer to an ice cream maker and freeze according to manufacturer's instructions. Add cherries in the last 5 minutes of freezing and let machine stir them in.

Marshmallow Ice Cream

SERVES 8

This ice cream requires you to whip the cream before folding it into the mixture. The result is fluffy marshmallow madness.

2	eggs	2
2 tbsp	granulated sugar	25 mL
2 cups	milk	500 mL
1	bag (8 oz/250 g) large marshmallows (about 40)	1
2 tbsp	vanilla	25 mL
2 cups	whipping (35%) cream	500 mL

1. In a bowl, whisk eggs with sugar until thickened and pale yellow. Set aside.

2. In a medium saucepan over medium-low heat, bring milk to a simmer. Add marshmallows and stir until melted, being careful not to burn them. Gradually whisk into the egg mixture.

3. Return entire mixture to the saucepan. Cook over low heat, stirring constantly, until the mixture is thick enough to coat the back of a wooden spoon. Be careful not to let it boil. Strain into a clean large bowl and stir in vanilla. Let cool to room temperature.

4. In a large bowl, whip whipping cream until firm peaks form. Gently fold into the cooled custard mixture. Cover and refrigerate until completely cold or overnight.

5. Stir cream mixture. Transfer to an ice cream maker and freeze according to manufacturer's instructions.

Rice Krispies Square Marshmallow Ice Cream

SERVES 8 TO 10

If you like snacking on Rice Krispies squares, you'll love this ice cream. One taste and you are transported back to snack time at grade school. The key is to add the chopped squares just moments before finishing the freezing — otherwise, they turn into a mushy mess.

2	eggs	2
2 tbsp	granulated sugar	25 mL
2 cups	milk	500 mL
1	bag (8 oz/250 g) large marshmallows (about 40) or 2 cups (500 mL) store-bought marshmallow spread (fluff)	1
2 tbsp	vanilla	25 mL
2 cups	whipping (35%) cream	500 mL
2 cups	chopped Rice Krispies squares (store-bought will do)	500 mL

1. In a bowl, whisk eggs with sugar until thickened and pale yellow. Set aside.

2. In a medium saucepan over medium-low heat, bring milk to a simmer. Add marshmallows and stir until melted, being careful not to burn them. Gradually whisk into the egg mixture.

3. Return entire mixture to the saucepan. Cook over low heat, stirring constantly, until the mixture is thick enough to coat the back of a wooden spoon. Be careful not to let it boil. Strain into a clean large bowl and stir in vanilla. Let cool to room temperature.

4. In a large bowl, whip whipping cream until firm peaks form. Gently fold into the cooled custard mixture. Cover and refrigerate until completely cold or overnight.

5. Stir cream mixture. Transfer to an ice cream maker and freeze according to manufacturer's instructions. Add Rice Krispies squares in the last 5 minutes of freezing and let machine stir them in.

S'mores Ice Cream

SERVES 8 TO 10

The campfire experience would be even better if you switched up the traditional s'mores and served s'mores ice cream instead. Even if you have no plans for camping out, this dessert is worth making. The secret is roasting the marshmallows. The preferred method is with a stick and an open flame, but an oven will do just fine.

• Baking sheet, lined with greased foil

2	eggs	2
1 cup	granulated sugar	250 mL
2 cups	milk	500 mL
2 cups	whipping (35%) cream	500 mL
1	bag (8 oz/250 g) mini marshmallows (about 2 cups/ 500 mL)	1
1 cup	broken graham crackers	250 mL
1 cup	chopped milk chocolate	250 mL

1. In a bowl, whisk eggs with sugar until thickened and pale yellow. Set aside.

2. In a medium saucepan over medium-low heat, bring milk to a simmer. Gradually whisk into the egg mixture.

3. Return entire mixture to the saucepan. Cook over low heat, stirring constantly, until the mixture is thick enough to coat the back of a wooden spoon. Be careful not to let it boil. Strain into a clean large bowl. Let cool to room temperature.

4. Stir in whipping cream and vanilla. Cover and refrigerate until completely cold or overnight.

5. Preheat broiler. Place marshmallows on prepared baking sheet and broil until lightly toasted, making sure they don't burn. Let cool.

6. Stir cream mixture. Transfer to an ice cream maker and freeze according to manufacturer's instructions. Add marshmallows, graham crackers and chocolate in the last 5 minutes of freezing and let machine stir them in.

Garbage Pail Ice Cream

SERVES 8

Created one Sunday afternoon, this ice cream is about cleaning out your baking cupboard. Throw in anything you think works, flavor-wise. We found maraschino cherries, chopped pecans, sweetened coconut and chocolate syrup. You could add cereal, cookies, nuts, chocolate chips — the ideas are limitless.

2	egg yolks	2
1/2 cup	granulated sugar	125 mL
2 cups	milk	500 mL
1 cup	chocolate syrup	250 mL
2 cups	whipping (35%) cream	500 mL
1 tbsp	vanilla	15 mL
1 cup	chopped drained maraschino cherries	250 mL
1/2 cup	chopped pecans	125 mL
1/2 cup	sweetened shredded coconut	125 mL

1. In a bowl, whisk egg yolks with sugar until thickened and pale yellow. Set aside.

2. In a medium saucepan over medium-low heat, bring milk and chocolate syrup to a simmer. Gradually whisk into the egg mixture.

3. Return entire mixture to the saucepan. Cook over low heat, stirring constantly, until the mixture is thick enough to coat the back of a wooden spoon. Be careful not to let it boil. Strain into a clean large bowl. Let cool to room temperature.

4. Stir in whipping cream and vanilla. Cover and refrigerate until completely cold or overnight.

5. Stir cream mixture. Transfer to an ice cream maker and freeze according to manufacturer's instructions. Add cherries, pecans and coconut in the last 5 minutes of freezing and let machine stir them in.

Gelatos

Chocolate Gelato

¼ cup	granulated sugar	50 mL
3 tbsp	cornstarch	45 mL
Pinch	salt	Pinch
3 cups	milk, divided	750 mL
2	bars (each 3½ oz/100 g) bittersweet chocolate, broken into small pieces	2

1. In a bowl, whisk together sugar, cornstarch, salt and ¼ cup (50 mL) of the milk. Set aside.

2. In a heavy saucepan, bring 2 cups (500 mL) of the milk to a boil over medium heat. Gradually whisk in sugar mixture and return to a boil, whisking constantly. Cook, whisking frequently, until sugar is dissolved, about 4 minutes. Remove from heat.

3. Place chocolate in a bowl. In a small saucepan, bring the remaining ¾ cup (175 mL) milk to a boil. Pour over chocolate and whisk gently until chocolate is melted, about 1 minute. Stir into the sugar-milk mixture. Cover and refrigerate until completely cold or overnight.

4. Stir milk mixture. Transfer to an ice cream maker and freeze according to manufacturer's instructions.

Chocolate Chip Coffee Gelato

This gelato pleases both the coffee lover and the chocoholic. If you're really addicted to coffee, double the coffee granules for a real kick.

Serving suggestion:
Sprinkle 2 tsp (10 mL) sliced almonds, chopped hazelnuts or chopped pecans over each serving.

2 cups	milk, divided	500 mL
2 tbsp	cornstarch	25 mL
⅓ cup	granulated sugar	75 mL
3 tbsp	unsweetened cocoa powder	45 mL
1½ tbsp	instant coffee granules	22 mL
1 tbsp	vanilla	15 mL
2 oz	bittersweet chocolate, finely chopped, divided	60 g

1. In a small bowl, whisk ½ cup (125 mL) milk with cornstarch until smooth. Set aside.

2. In a medium saucepan over medium heat, whisk together remaining milk, sugar and cocoa powder. Bring to a simmer, stirring often. Whisk in coffee granules. Whisk the cornstarch mixture to recombine. Gradually whisk into sugar mixture. Return to a boil, stirring often. Strain into a clean large bowl. Let cool to room temperature.

3. Stir in vanilla and half of the chocolate. Cover and refrigerate until completely cold or overnight.

4. Stir milk mixture. Transfer to an ice cream maker and freeze according to manufacturer's instructions. Add remaining chocolate during last 5 minutes of freezing and let machine stir it in.

Vanilla Gelato

SERVES 4 TO 6

On a hot summer day in Italy, you'll find most people leisurely licking a gelato. If you're going to make gelato from scratch, go for vanilla. But don't try to substitute something lighter for the whipping cream. As this gelato doesn't have an egg-custard base, we found that whipping cream made it rich and smooth. It's an easy recipe that's very satisfying — and one with many add-in possibilities.

1	vanilla bean	1
2 cups	milk	500 mL
1 cup	whipping (35%) cream	250 mL
¾ cup	granulated sugar	175 mL

1. Slit vanilla bean lengthwise and scrape seeds into a medium saucepan. Add vanilla pod, milk, cream and sugar. Place saucepan over medium-low heat. Cook, stirring occasionally, until sugar is dissolved. Bring to a simmer. Strain into a clean large bowl, discarding vanilla pod. Let cool to room temperature.

2. Cover and refrigerate until completely cold or overnight.

3. Stir cream mixture. Transfer to an ice cream maker and freeze according to manufacturer's instructions.

❧ Variation
Chocolate Almond Gelato: Add ½ cup (125 mL) chocolate-covered almonds in the last 5 minutes of freezing and let machine stir them in.

Mascarpone Vanilla Gelato with Pine Nuts

SERVES 4 TO 6

A fragrant infusion made with a vanilla bean gives this recipe real panache. Let the nuts cool to room temperature before adding them to the semifrozen mixture.

Tip: Toast pine nuts just until golden in a toaster oven or dry skillet over medium-high heat. Whichever method you choose, keep stirring the nuts, as they can burn quickly. Let cool to room temperature before adding them to the machine.

1 cup	milk	250 mL
1 cup	whipping (35%) cream	250 mL
½ cup	granulated sugar	125 mL
1	vanilla bean	1
1 cup	mascarpone cheese	250 mL
⅓ cup	toasted pine nuts (see Tip, left)	75 mL
1 tbsp	lemon zest	15 mL

1. In a medium saucepan over medium heat, combine milk, cream and sugar. Simmer, stirring, until sugar is dissolved and bubbles form around the edge of the saucepan. Remove from heat.

2. Slit vanilla bean lengthwise. Scrape seeds into the milk mixture. Add vanilla pod. Let stand for 30 minutes. Strain into a clean large bowl, discarding vanilla pod. Cover and refrigerate until completely cold or overnight.

3. Stir in mascarpone cheese, pine nuts and lemon zest. Transfer to an ice cream maker and freeze according to manufacturer's instructions.

Zabaglione Gelato

2 cups	milk	500 mL
4	egg yolks	4
1/2 cup	granulated sugar	125 mL
1/3 cup	Marsala wine	75 mL
1 tbsp	lemon zest	15 mL

1. In the top half of a double boiler without the heat on, combine milk, egg yolks and sugar, stirring, until thoroughly blended.

2. Place top half of double boiler over bottom saucepan of simmering water. Whisk for 3 minutes or until thickened. Add Marsala wine and lemon zest and continue whisking for a few minutes more.

3. Remove top half of double boiler from bottom. Strain into a clean large bowl. Let cool to room temperature. Cover and refrigerate until completely cold or overnight.

4. Stir milk mixture. Transfer to an ice cream maker and freeze according to manufacturer's instructions.

❧ Variation

You can make a Spanish-inspired gelato by substituting amontillado sherry for the Marsala wine and, at the last minute, adding 1 tbsp (15 mL) orange zest and 1/2 tsp (2 mL) ground cinnamon along with the lemon zest.

Cinnamon Gelato

4	egg yolks	4
1 cup	granulated sugar	250 mL
3 cups	milk	750 mL
3	cinnamon sticks, broken into pieces	3
1	bay leaf	1

1. In a bowl, whisk egg yolks with sugar until thickened and pale yellow. Set aside.

2. In a medium saucepan over medium heat, bring milk, cinnamon sticks and bay leaf to a simmer. Cook for 10 minutes. Remove from heat and let stand for 15 minutes. Strain into a clean large bowl, discarding cinnamon sticks and bay leaf. Gradually whisk into the egg mixture.

3. Return entire mixture to the saucepan. Cook over low heat, stirring constantly, until the mixture is thick enough to coat the back of a wooden spoon. Be careful not to let it boil. Let cool to room temperature. Cover and refrigerate until completely cold or overnight.

4. Stir milk mixture. Transfer to an ice cream maker and freeze according to manufacturer's instructions.

Variation

Chocolate Peanut Butter Cinnamon Gelato: Chop 6 chocolate peanut butter cups into small pieces and add in the last 5 minutes of freezing. Allow chocolate peanut butter cups to mix in slightly.

Raspberry Cassis Gelato

For the raspberry lover's dream dessert, we layer small scoops of this gelato with fresh berries in an old-fashioned sundae glass and top with a dollop of freshly whipped cream.

Tip: Take care not to overcook the custard or the eggs will scramble.

4 cups	fresh raspberries	1 L
1 cup	granulated sugar, divided	250 mL
1/2 cup	water	125 mL
2 tbsp	black currant–flavored liqueur or black currant syrup	25 mL
4	egg yolks	4
2 cups	milk	500 mL
1 cup	whipping (35%) cream	250 mL
1 tsp	vanilla	5 mL

1. In a medium saucepan, combine raspberries, 1/2 cup (125 mL) of the sugar and the water; bring to a boil. Reduce heat and simmer for 10 minutes, or until fruit is soft. Remove from heat and let stand for 10 minutes. Using the back of a wooden spoon, press through a fine sieve into a bowl to remove seeds. Stir in liqueur. Let cool or cover and refrigerate overnight.

2. Meanwhile, in a bowl, whisk egg yolks with the remaining sugar until thickened and pale yellow. Set aside.

3. In a clean medium saucepan over medium-low heat, bring milk and cream to a simmer. Gradually whisk into the egg mixture.

4. Return entire mixture to the saucepan. Cook over low heat, stirring constantly, until the mixture is thick enough to coat the back of a wooden spoon. Be careful not to let it boil. Strain into a clean large bowl. Let cool to room temperature.

5. Stir in vanilla. Cover and refrigerate until completely cold or overnight.

6. Stir raspberry mixture into the custard. Transfer to an ice cream maker and freeze according to manufacturer's instructions.

Strawberry Gelato

SERVES 6 TO 8

Gelato is popular not only for its intense flavor and color but also because it's lighter than traditional ice cream. This one calls for milk but no cream.

4	egg yolks	4
1 cup	granulated sugar	250 mL
2 cups	milk	500 mL
2 cups	puréed strawberries, about 3 cups (750 mL) whole strawberries	500 mL
½ tsp	vanilla	2 mL

1. In a bowl, whisk egg yolks with sugar until thickened and pale yellow. Set aside.

2. In a medium saucepan over medium heat, bring milk to a simmer, stirring occasionally. Gradually whisk into the egg mixture.

3. Return entire mixture to the saucepan. Cook over low heat, stirring often, until the mixture is thick enough to coat the back of a wooden spoon. Be careful not to let it boil. Strain into a clean large bowl. Let cool to room temperature.

4. Stir in strawberry purée and vanilla. Cover and refrigerate until completely cold or overnight.

5. Stir milk mixture. Transfer to an ice cream maker and freeze according to manufacturer's instructions.

Variation

Strawberry Balsamic Gelato: Balsamic vinegar splashed on strawberries is a wonderful surprise. The same can be said for the above recipe when you stir in 1 tbsp (15 mL) aged balsamic vinegar along with the strawberry purée.

Grape Gelato

SERVES 8 TO 10

Although this gelato doesn't turn the color of a fine Merlot, its pinkish hue has eye appeal. Pour a little cassis syrup over each serving for extra flavor.

4	egg yolks	4
¾ cup	granulated sugar, divided	175 mL
3 cups	milk	750 mL
2 lbs	seedless red grapes	1 kg
1 cup	white grape juice	250 mL

1. In a bowl, whisk egg yolks with 6 tbsp (90 mL) sugar until thickened and pale yellow. Set aside

2. In a medium saucepan over medium-low heat, heat milk until bubbles appear around the edge. Gradually whisk into egg mixture, stirring constantly.

3. Return entire mixture to the saucepan. Cook over low heat, stirring constantly, until the mixture is thick enough to coat the back of a wooden spoon. Be careful not to let it boil. Strain into a clean large bowl. Let cool to room temperature. Cover and refrigerate until completely cold or overnight.

4. Meanwhile, in a separate saucepan over medium-low heat, cook grapes, juice and remaining sugar, stirring occasionally, until mixture is thickened. Let cool.

5. In a food processor or blender, purée grape mixture with chilled custard until smooth.

6. Transfer to an ice cream maker and freeze according to manufacturer's instructions.

Pear Ginger Ricotta Gelato

Ricotta cheese is a great way to add creaminess to gelato. Here, it's partnered with pears and crystallized ginger to make an elegant frozen dessert. We found that canned pears packed in unsweetened juice added more flavor than fresh ones. You can always serve a scoop of this gelato with a poached pear to heighten the flavor.

Tip: Do not add pears to the hot mixture — the heat will turn the pears to mush.

3 cups	milk	750 mL
2 cups	ricotta cheese	500 mL
½ cup	granulated sugar	125 mL
¼ cup	crystallized ginger, chopped	50 mL
¼ tsp	vanilla	1 mL
1	cinnamon stick	1
1	can (14 oz/398 mL) pear halves in unsweetened juice	1

1. In a medium saucepan over medium heat, whisk together milk, ricotta cheese, sugar, ginger, vanilla and cinnamon stick. Bring just to a boil. Strain into a clean large bowl, discarding cinnamon stick. Let cool to room temperature.

2. Drain pears, reserving 3 tbsp (45 mL) juice. Chop pears. Stir pears into milk mixture along with reserved juice (see Tip, left). Cover and refrigerate until completely cold or overnight.

3. Stir milk mixture. Transfer to an ice cream maker and freeze according to manufacturer's instructions.

Variations

Peach Ginger Ricotta Gelato: Substitute 1 can (14 oz/ 398 mL) peach halves and 3 tbsp (45 mL) peach juice from can for the pears and pear juice.

Lemon Ginger Ricotta Gelato: Omit pears and juice. Add zest of 1 lemon and 3 tbsp (45 mL) freshly squeezed lemon juice.

Honeyed Yellow Plum and Crème Fraîche Gelato

SERVES 6

Only a small amount of crème fraîche is used, but the result is creamy and delicious — not too sweet and not too rich.

2 cups	roughly chopped yellow plums (8 to 10)	500 mL
2 tbsp	dry white wine, such as Chardonnay (optional)	25 mL
2 tbsp	liquid honey	25 mL
½ cup	Simple Syrup (see recipe, page 20)	125 mL
½ cup	crème fraîche	125 mL

1. In a medium, heavy saucepan, combine plums, wine (if using) and honey; cook over low heat for 30 minutes, or until plums are soft. Remove from heat and let cool.

2. Transfer plums to a food processor or blender. Add syrup and purée until smooth.

3. Transfer to an ice cream maker and freeze according to manufacturer's instructions. At the semifrozen stage, add crème fraîche and continue freezing.

✿ Variations

Yellow Plum and Sake Gelato: Substitute Japanese rice wine (sake) for the dry white wine.

Just for Kids Yellow Plum Ice Pops: Omit the wine. In Step 3, instead of using the ice cream maker, divide plum mixture among ice-pop molds and freeze until slushy. Insert sticks. Return to freezer and freeze until firm.

Kiwi Gelato

SERVES 4 TO 6

Though often used to make ices, kiwifruit also makes a novel but yummy ice cream. Whether you use green kiwifruits or the new gold variety, it's essential that they be very ripe and soft when squeezed.

5	large kiwifruits, peeled and sliced	5
½ cup	Simple Syrup (see recipe, page 20)	125 mL
½ cup	milk	125 mL
¼ cup	whipping (35%) cream	50 mL
½ tsp	vanilla	2 mL

1. In a food processor or blender, purée kiwifruits with syrup until smooth.

2. Add milk, cream and vanilla. Pulse until well blended. Pour into a clean large bowl (do not strain). Cover and refrigerate until completely cold.

3. Stir milk mixture. Transfer to an ice cream maker and freeze according to manufacturer's instructions.

Variation

Kiwi Candied Ginger Gelato: Add ¼ cup (50 mL) finely chopped candied ginger to the ice cream maker in the last 5 minutes of freezing and let the machine stir it in.

Kiwi Basics

What looks like a fuzzy brown egg is really an excellent source of vitamin C. One large kiwi provides about 80 mg of vitamin C.

Passion Fruit Gelato

SERVES 4 TO 6

Fresh fruit is always a good way to add flavor to frozen desserts, so take advantage of what's in season. This gelato features passion fruit to give it a sweet-tart taste and an orangish hue.

Serving suggestion:
Serve a scoop of Passion Fruit Gelato with a fresh fruit salad or puréed passion fruit.

4	egg yolks	4
1/2 cup	granulated sugar	125 mL
2 cups	milk	500 mL
4	passion fruits	4
1 tsp	vanilla	5 mL

1. In a bowl, whisk egg yolks with sugar until thickened and pale yellow. Set aside.

2. In a medium saucepan over medium-low heat, bring milk to a simmer, stirring occasionally. Gradually whisk into egg mixture.

3. Return entire mixture to the saucepan. Cook over low heat, stirring often, until the mixture is thick enough to coat the back of a wooden spoon. Be careful not to let it boil. Strain into a clean large bowl. Let cool to room temperature. Cover and refrigerate until completely cold or overnight.

4. Remove pulp and seeds from passion fruits to make about 1 cup (250 mL). Stir into milk mixture along with vanilla.

5. Transfer to an ice cream maker and freeze according to manufacturer's instructions.

Variation
Raspberry–Passion Fruit Gelato: Add 1/4 cup (50 mL) puréed raspberries along with passion fruit pulp and seeds before freezing.

Pineapple Mint Gelato

1	small ripe pineapple	1
4	egg yolks	4
1/2 cup	granulated sugar	125 mL
2 cups	milk	500 mL
1 tsp	vanilla	5 mL
2 tbsp	chopped fresh mint (see Tips, left and page 184)	25 mL

1. Peel and core pineapple and cut into chunks to make 2 cups (500 mL). In a food processor or blender, purée until smooth. Set aside.

2. In a bowl, whisk egg yolks with sugar until thickened and pale yellow. Set aside.

3. In a medium saucepan over medium-low heat, bring milk to a simmer, stirring occasionally. Gradually whisk into the egg mixture.

4. Return entire mixture to the saucepan. Cook over low heat, stirring often, until the mixture is thick enough to coat the back of a wooden spoon. Be careful not to let it boil. Strain into a clean large bowl. Let cool to room temperature. Cover and refrigerate until completely cold or overnight.

5. Stir in vanilla and pineapple purée. Transfer to an ice cream maker and freeze according to manufacturer's instructions. Just before serving, sprinkle with mint.

Variations

Tropical Gelato: Add 1 banana, mashed, to the custard mixture.

Pineapple Orange Gelato: Omit mint. Stir in grated zest and juice of 1 orange along with the pineapple.

Persimmon Gelato

3	fresh persimmons, peeled	3
1 cup	Simple Syrup (see recipe, page 20)	250 mL
1 cup	whipping (35%) cream	250 mL
1 tsp	orange zest	5 mL

1. In a food processor or blender, purée persimmons with syrup until smooth. Transfer to a clean bowl.

2. In a separate bowl, whip cream. Fold into persimmon mixture. Stir in orange zest. Cover and refrigerate until completely cold or overnight.

3. Transfer to an ice cream maker and freeze according to manufacturer's instructions.

Persimmon Basics

The national fruit of Japan also has a North American history, in that Native Americans taught European settlers how to use the fruit in breads and puddings. Persimmons are ready to eat when they are ultra-soft. Just break the skin and spoon out the delicious flesh.

Fig Gelato

SERVES 6

A few ingredients and a food processor — how easy is that? Plus, you get an unusual gelato that is reminiscent of a dessert from the hills of Tuscany. It's equally good on its own or paired with sliced oranges or plain honey cake.

4 oz	dried Mission figs	125 g
½ cup	mascarpone cheese	125 mL
1 tbsp	orange-flavored liqueur	15 mL
2 tbsp	liquid honey	25 mL
1½ cups	milk	375 mL

1. In a food processor, finely chop figs. Add mascarpone, liqueur and honey; purée until smooth. Add milk and process for a few seconds, just to combine.

2. Transfer to an ice cream maker and freeze according to manufacturer's instructions.

Variation

Fig Almond Gelato: Substitute 1 tsp (5 mL) almond extract for the orange-flavored liqueur.

Salted Pistachio Gelato

We toasted these pistachios to make this very nutty, scrumptious dessert.

Tip: This recipe contains raw egg whites. If the food safety of raw eggs is a concern for you, use the pasteurized liquid egg whites instead.

1 cup	toasted salted shelled pistachios	250 mL
1 cup	granulated sugar, divided	250 mL
4	egg whites or ½ cup (125 mL) pasteurized liquid egg whites	4
1½ cups	chilled whipping (35%) cream	375 mL
½ cup	milk	125 mL
¼ tsp	rose water	1 mL

1. In a food processor, pulse pistachios and half the sugar until coarsely ground.

2. In a bowl, beat egg whites until they hold soft peaks. Beat in the remaining sugar, a little at a time, and continue to beat until the meringue is glossy and holds stiff peaks.

3. In a medium bowl, combine whipping cream, milk and rose water. Gently fold in the meringue and the sugared pistachios.

4. Transfer to an ice cream maker and freeze according to manufacturer's instructions.

❧ Variation
You can substitute almond extract for the rose water, if you prefer.

Honey Walnut Gelato

You can vary the taste of this dessert by experimenting with different types of honey, though orange-blossom is a particular favorite.

3	egg yolks	3
1/2 cup	liquid honey	125 mL
1 1/2 cups	milk	375 mL
1/2 cup	whipping (35%) cream	125 mL
1 tsp	vanilla	5 mL
1/4 cup	toasted chopped walnuts	50 mL

1. In a bowl, whisk egg yolks with honey until thickened and pale yellow. Set aside.

2. In a medium saucepan over medium-low heat, bring milk and cream to a simmer. Gradually whisk into the egg mixture.

3. Return entire mixture to the saucepan. Cook over low heat, stirring constantly, until the mixture is thick enough to coat the back of a wooden spoon. Be careful not to let it boil. Strain into a clean large bowl. Let cool to room temperature.

4. Stir in vanilla and walnuts. Cover and refrigerate until completely cold or overnight

5. Stir cream mixture. Transfer to an ice cream maker and freeze according to manufacturer's instructions.

Bubble Gelato

SERVES 6

Inspired by both a childhood love of tapioca pudding and a fascination with the bubble tea that's so popular in Asian tea shops, we created an easy milk-based gelato that all ages seem to adore. You can buy instant tapioca in any supermarket. Anyone on a gluten-free diet can enjoy this treat.

3 cups	milk	750 mL
½ cup	granulated sugar	125 mL
3 tbsp	instant tapioca granules	45 mL
1	egg	1
1 tbsp	vanilla	15 mL
	Zest of 1 lemon	

1. In a medium saucepan without the heat on, whisk together milk, sugar, tapioca and egg. Let stand for 3 minutes. Place saucepan over medium heat and bring to a boil, stirring constantly. Transfer to a bowl (do not strain).

2. Stir in vanilla and lemon zest. Let cool to room temperature. Cover and refrigerate until completely cold or overnight.

3. Stir milk mixture. Transfer to an ice cream maker and freeze according to manufacturer's instructions.

Ices, Sorbets & Granitas

continued on next page…

Chocolate Ice

½ cup	granulated sugar	125 mL
¼ cup	unsweetened cocoa powder	50 mL
3 oz	bittersweet chocolate, finely chopped	90 g
1 tbsp	orange zest	15 mL
¼ cup	freshly squeezed orange juice	50 mL

SERVES 4

This is a good example of how a recipe is so much more than just the sum of its parts. The ingredients would seem to add up to frozen chocolate water, but the result is an exquisite dessert that you will make over and over again. The trick is the quality of chocolate used — we used Lindt 70% dark chocolate — so don't make this with the traditional baking variety.

1. In a medium saucepan over medium heat, bring 2 cups (500 mL) water, sugar and cocoa powder to a boil, whisking constantly.

2. Reduce heat and simmer for 1 minute or until sugar is dissolved and cocoa is well blended. Stir in chopped chocolate until melted. Remove from heat and transfer to a bowl. Let cool to room temperature.

3. Stir in orange zest and juice. Cover and refrigerate until completely cold or overnight.

4. Stir chocolate mixture. Transfer to an ice cream maker and freeze according to manufacturer's instructions.

Berry Spiced Tea Ice

When berries are abundant, combine them with tea and spices for an exotic and sophisticated twist. Use a full-bodied tea, such as oolong.

1 cup	blackberries	250 mL
1 cup	Simple Syrup (see recipe, page 20)	250 mL
½ cup	raspberries	125 mL
½ cup	cold strong tea	125 mL
1 tbsp	freshly squeezed lemon juice	15 mL
½ tsp	ground cinnamon	2 mL
Pinch	ground nutmeg	Pinch
Pinch	freshly ground black pepper	Pinch

1. In a food processor or blender, purée blackberries, syrup, raspberries and tea until smooth. Using the back of a wooden spoon, press through a fine sieve into a bowl to remove seeds.

2. Stir in lemon juice, cinnamon, nutmeg and pepper. Cover and refrigerate until completely cold or overnight.

3. Stir berry mixture. Transfer to an ice cream maker and freeze according to manufacturer's instructions.

Blackberry Cabernet Ice

3 cups	fresh blackberries	750 mL
2 cups	Simple Syrup (see recipe, page 20)	500 mL
¼ cup	Cabernet Sauvignon wine	50 mL
1 tsp	freshly squeezed lemon juice	5 mL

This simple-to-make ice, with its deep color, is exquisite to look at and perfect for elegant dining during the summer, when these fruits are at their most luscious. You can use any full-bodied dry red wine and increase the amount of wine slightly — just remember that the more alcohol you add, the less the ice will freeze.

1. In a food processor or blender, in batches if necessary, purée blackberries, syrup, wine and lemon juice until smooth. Using the back of a wooden spoon, press through a fine sieve into a bowl to remove seeds. Cover and refrigerate until completely cold or overnight.

2. Stir berry mixture. Transfer to an ice cream maker and freeze according to manufacturer's instructions.

Variation
Blueberry Zinfandel Ice: Substitute blueberries for the blackberries and white Zinfandel for the Cabernet Sauvignon.

Blueberry Ginger Ice

It seems not to matter whether you use fresh or thawed frozen blueberries in this recipe. You can omit the chopped mint if you prefer. For a perfect red, white and blue holiday dessert, serve a scoop of this ice with a scoop of vanilla ice cream and a scoop of raspberry ice.

Tip: When using herbs, make sure they have not been treated with pesticides. Treat herbs to a light wash in soapy water and rinse very well.

2 cups	blueberries	500 mL
1 cup	Simple Syrup (see recipe, page 20)	250 mL
2 tbsp	grated gingerroot	25 mL
2 tbsp	freshly squeezed lime juice	25 mL
1 tbsp	finely chopped fresh mint (see Tip, left)	15 mL
1 tbsp	freshly squeezed lemon juice	15 mL

1. In a food processor or blender, purée blueberries, syrup, ginger, lime juice, mint and lemon juice until smooth. Transfer to a bowl. Cover and refrigerate until completely cold or overnight.

2. Stir berry mixture. Transfer to an ice cream maker and freeze according to manufacturer's instructions.

Variation
Blueberry Ginger Zinfandel Ice: Add $\frac{1}{2}$ cup (125 mL) white Zinfandel wine to mixture before chilling.

Blueberry Honeydew Melon Ice

SERVES 6

The ready availability of blueberry juice means you can make this ice any time of year. Ginger cookies are a welcome addition, either crumbled on top or served on the side.

½	honeydew melon, seeded and chopped into small pieces (about 2 cups/500 mL)	½
1 cup	Simple Syrup (see recipe, page 20)	250 mL
1 cup	unsweetened blueberry juice	250 mL

1. In a food processor or blender, purée melon and syrup until smooth. Transfer to a bowl and stir in blueberry juice. Cover and refrigerate until completely cold or overnight.

2. Stir fruit mixture. Transfer to an ice cream maker and freeze according to manufacturer's instructions.

Cranberry Sorbet

This sorbet is a little more substantial than ones traditionally made with just cranberry juice. If you want to cut down on the calories, you can use artificially sweetened juice instead of the Simple Syrup. If you cut back on the sugar syrup and increase the lemon juice to taste, you can concoct a lively palate-cleansing ice for a formal Christmas or New Year's dinner.

2 cups	unsweetened cranberry juice	500 mL
$\frac{1}{2}$ cup	dried cranberries	125 mL
1 cup	Simple Syrup (see recipe, page 20)	250 mL
$\frac{1}{4}$ cup	orange juice	50 mL
1 tbsp	freshly squeezed lemon juice	15 mL

1. In a bowl, stir cranberry juice with dried cranberries. Let stand for 1 hour or until cranberries are plump.

2. Stir in syrup, orange juice and lemon juice. Cover and refrigerate until completely cold or overnight.

3. Stir cranberry mixture. Transfer to an ice cream maker and freeze according to manufacturer's instructions.

Raspberry Vinegar Ice

For those of us who don't have a sweet tooth, this intense fruit ice has a definite zing to it. Experiment by using different kinds of vinegar — balsamic or ice wine, for example.

2 cups	fresh raspberries	500 mL
½ cup	granulated sugar	125 mL
1 tbsp	raspberry vinegar	15 mL

1. In a medium, heavy saucepan, bring berries and sugar to a boil, stirring, until sugar is dissolved. Reduce heat and simmer, stirring occasionally, for about 20 minutes or until fruit is very soft.

2. Using the back of a wooden spoon, press through a fine sieve into a bowl to remove seeds. Stir in vinegar. Let cool. Cover and refrigerate until completely cold or overnight.

3. Stir raspberry mixture. Transfer to an ice cream maker and freeze according to manufacturer's instructions.

Santa Fe Raspberry Lime Ice

This ice, with its flavor of berries enriched with a hit of lime, shakes up your taste buds and the conversation with its Southwest nod to the chili pepper. Enjoy it as a palate cleanser between courses or as a dessert paired with chocolate chip cookies or brownies. Tone down the fire, stoke it up or leave the pepper out altogether.

Tip: Pickled jalapeños work just fine in this recipe. If you're using a fresh pepper, use a medium-hot pepper and wear kitchen gloves to avoid burning your skin. Remove the seeds and ribs, then chop finely.

Serving suggestion: Serve Santa Fe Raspberry Lime Ice in a martini glass rimmed with tequila and granulated sugar.

1 ½ cups	raspberries, fresh or frozen	375 mL
1 cup	Simple Syrup (see recipe, page 20)	250 mL
	Zest and juice of 2 limes	
½ tsp	finely chopped jalapeño pepper (see Tip, left)	2 mL

1. In a food processor or blender, purée raspberries with syrup until smooth.

2. Using the back of a wooden spoon, press through a fine sieve into a bowl to remove seeds. Stir in lime zest and juice and jalapeño pepper. Cover and refrigerate until completely cold or overnight.

3. Stir raspberry mixture. Transfer to an ice cream maker and freeze according to manufacturer's instructions.

❧ Variation
Minty Raspberry Lime Ice: To capture the essence of summer, replace the pepper with 2 tbsp (25 mL) chopped fresh mint.

Strawberry Pineapple Sorbet

SERVES 4 TO 6

Try this low-calorie fruity sorbet, especially if you or your guests are on a sugar-restricted diet.

3 cups	chopped strawberries	750 mL
3/4 cup	pineapple juice	175 mL
1/2	large banana	1/2
1/4	water	50 mL

1. In a food processor or blender, purée strawberries, pineapple juice, banana and water until smooth. Transfer to a bowl. Cover and refrigerate until completely cold or overnight.

2. Stir fruit mixture. Transfer to an ice cream maker and freeze according to manufacturer's instructions.

Sour Cherry Sorbet

*With its vibrant ruby
color and its tangy
taste, this can be served
year-round thanks to
bottled sour cherries.*

¾ cup	Simple Syrup (see recipe, page 20)	175 mL
1	jar (19 oz/540 mL) pitted red sour cherries in light syrup	1
	Juice of 1 lemon	

1. In a food processor or blender, purée syrup, cherries with syrup and lemon juice until smooth. Transfer to a bowl. Cover and refrigerate until completely cold or overnight.

2. Stir cherry mixture. Transfer to an ice cream maker and freeze according to manufacturer's instructions.

Variation

For added zing, mix in 1 tbsp (15 mL) Zinfandel wine in the last 10 minutes of freezing.

Apple Muscat Ice

This idea came to us from Jacques and Lynn Bernier, who remember it as an all-time favorite. To ensure this tantalizing ice achieves a stable frozen state, we recommend that you make it with a low-alcohol Muscat wine, such as the 5.5% alcohol Moscato D'Asti. This is definitely a festive ice, perfect for entertaining and suitable as either a palate cleanser between courses or a frozen accompaniment to either fresh fruit or something devilishly chocolate. You may even choose to grate the apples unpeeled for extra color.

Serving suggestion: This is a great light dessert to complement a cheese-and-fruit platter.

3	Granny Smith apples, peeled and grated	3
1 tbsp	freshly squeezed lemon juice	15 mL
1 cup	Simple Syrup (see recipe, page 20)	250 mL
1 cup	low-alcohol Muscat wine	250 mL
2 tbsp	liquid honey	25 mL
½ tsp	grated gingerroot	2 mL

1. In a bowl, toss apples with lemon juice. Stir in syrup, wine, honey and ginger. Cover and refrigerate until completely cold or overnight.

2. Stir apple mixture. Transfer to an ice cream maker and freeze according to manufacturer's instructions.

Pear Cardamom Sorbet

Cardamom, a spice popular in Indian cuisine, is paired with pears for a unique, agreeable taste. We especially recommend this ice after a meal of curry. Because we use canned pears, this sorbet is easy to make any time of year.

Serving suggestion: The French term *trou normand* is roughly translated as "Norman hole" and is popular in the region of Normandy as a dessert sorbet splashed with an *eau-de-vie*. To make your own, use the bottom of a coffee spoon to press a hole into the center of a scoop of Pear Cardamom Sorbet, then fill the hole with a pear eau-de-vie or brandy of your choice.

1 cup	Simple Syrup (see recipe, page 20)	250 mL
2	cans (each 14 oz/398 mL) pears in syrup	2
2 tbsp	freshly squeezed lemon juice	25 mL
Pinch	ground cardamom	Pinch

1. In a food processor or blender, purée syrup, pears with syrup, lemon juice and cardamom until smooth. Transfer to a bowl. Cover and refrigerate until completely cold or overnight.

2. Stir pear mixture. Transfer to an ice cream maker and freeze according to manufacturer's instructions.

Variation
Pear Ginger Sorbet: Substitute 2 tbsp (25 mL) finely chopped crystallized ginger for the cardamom.

Chocolate Chip Coffee Gelato (page 161)

Grape Gelato (page 168)

Persimmon Gelato (page 174)

Star Anise and Mandarin Orange Ice (page 196)

Three-Layered Ice Cream Terrine

*For a special party, make a three-layered ice cream terrine
using Ginger Molasses Ice Cream, Lemon Ice Cream
and Pear Cardamom Sorbet.*

- 9- by 5-inch (2 L) loaf pan, lined with plastic wrap
  or waxed paper

2 cups	Ginger Molasses Ice Cream (see recipe, page 58)	500 mL
2 cups	Lemon Ice Cream (see recipe, page 81)	500 mL
2 cups	Pear Cardamom Sorbet (see recipe, page 192)	500 mL

1. Soften Ginger Molasses Ice Cream at room temperature
   for 15 minutes. Spread softened ice cream in prepared pan.
   Smooth top with a spatula. Freeze until firm.

2. Soften Lemon Ice Cream at room temperature for 15 minutes.
   Spread over first layer. Smooth top with a spatula. Freeze
   until firm.

3. Soften Pear Cardamom Sorbet at room temperature for
   15 minutes. Spread over second layer. Smooth top with a
   spatula. Cover with plastic wrap or waxed paper and freeze
   for 4 hours or until firm.

4. To serve, unwrap and turn out of pan onto cutting board.
   Peel off plastic wrap. Using a warm dry knife, cut into slices.

❧ **SERVES 6 TO 8**

Pear Cranberry Ice

We used canned pears for this easy dessert that celebrates winter and illustrates that cranberries are worth getting to know beyond Thanksgiving and Christmas. You can even omit the fresh cranberries and the honey for an easier "cupboard" version.

Tip: This recipe doubles well if you're making it for a larger group of guests or want extra on hand for the family.

1 cup	water	250 mL
½ cup	fresh cranberries	125 mL
1	can (14 oz/398 mL) pear halves in syrup	1
1½ cups	cranberry juice	375 mL
1 tbsp	liquid honey	15 mL

1. In a medium saucepan over high heat, cook water and fresh cranberries until the cranberries pop. Let cool.

2. In a food processor, purée pears with syrup until smooth.

3. Add cranberry mixture, cranberry juice and honey. Pulse for 30 seconds. Transfer to a clean large bowl. Cover and refrigerate until completely cold or overnight.

4. Stir pear mixture. Transfer to an ice cream maker and freeze according to manufacturer's instructions.

✿ Variation

If you prefer a taste that is more pear than cranberry or vice versa, play with the amounts. For a more intense pear flavor, use 2 cans of pears in syrup; for a more cranberry taste, double the amount of fresh cranberries to 1 cup (250 mL). Proceed with the recipe.

Mandarin Orange Ice

This is a quick, refreshing dessert to serve after a substantial meal. We make it during those months when mandarin oranges are not available fresh. Serve a scoop of it on a slice of dense chocolate cake.

4	cans (each 10 oz/284 mL) mandarin oranges in syrup	4
½ cup	granulated sugar	125 mL
¼ cup	freshly squeezed lemon juice	50 mL

1. In a food processor or blender, purée oranges with syrup, sugar and lemon juice until smooth. Transfer to a bowl. Cover and refrigerate until completely cold or overnight.

2. Stir orange mixture. Transfer to an ice cream maker and freeze according to manufacturer's instructions.

Star Anise and Mandarin Orange Ice

The licorice flavor of star anise adds a mellow edge to this Eastern-inspired ice. We like to serve this paired with plain vanilla ice cream or as a side to lemon loaf or angel food cake. Star anise vary in size, so you'll have to judge for yourself whether to use 6 or 8. Eight large star anise will produce an intense flavor.

Tip: For a faster version, use four 10-oz (284 mL) cans of mandarin oranges, drained.

2 cups	Simple Syrup (see recipe, page 20)	500 mL
6 to 8	whole star anise	6 to 8
20	mandarin oranges, peeled, pith and seeds removed	20

1. In a medium saucepan, bring syrup and star anise to a boil. Reduce heat and simmer for 3 minutes. Remove from heat and let steep for 30 minutes. Discard star anise.

2. In a food processor or blender, purée oranges until smooth. Using the back of a wooden spoon, press through a fine sieve into a bowl. Stir in anise-flavored syrup. Cover and refrigerate until completely cold or overnight.

3. Stir orange mixture. Transfer to an ice cream maker and freeze according to manufacturer's instructions.

Tequila Orange Granita

Great for a Mexican-themed party, this citrus-flavored granita can work not only as a refreshing dessert but also as a fun way to begin the party.

- 13- by 9-inch (3 L) metal baking pan

1 1/4 cups	water	300 mL
1/2 cup	granulated sugar	125 mL
	Juice of 7 oranges (about 2 1/3 cups/575 mL)	
6 tbsp	white tequila	90 mL
6	slices lime	6

1. In a bowl, stir together water, sugar, orange juice and tequila until sugar is dissolved.

2. Pour into baking pan and freeze for about 1 hour or until ice forms at the edges of the pan.

3. Using a fork, break up ice and stir to distribute frozen portions evenly. Freeze for 30 minutes or until solid.

4. Using a fork, stir to break up ice crystals. Continue freezing, stirring the mixture every 20 minutes, until slushy. Garnish with lime slices.

Tangerine Thyme Ice

Take advantage of bottled tangerine juice to make this easy, refreshing ice. A splash of vodka on each serving transforms it into a special between-courses palate cleanser.

Serving suggestion:
Pile this ice into chilled martini glasses. Top each with a sprig of fresh thyme.

2 cups	tangerine juice	500 mL
1 cup	Simple Syrup (see recipe, page 20)	250 mL
1 tsp	fresh thyme leaves	5 mL

1. In a medium bowl, combine tangerine juice, syrup and thyme; mix well. Cover and refrigerate until completely cold or overnight.

2. Stir juice mixture. Transfer to an ice cream maker and freeze according to manufacturer's instructions.

Grapefruit and Basil Slushy

SERVES 8

With fresh basil available year-round in supermarkets, you can easily make this a Sunday brunch starter, even in winter. In summer, we pour the mixture into molds, insert sticks and freeze to enjoy as icy pops — a tasty way to cool down.

	Grated zest of 2 large grapefruit	
	Juice of 4 large grapefruit	
2 cups	Simple Syrup (see recipe, page 20)	500 mL
2 tbsp	finely shredded fresh basil	25 mL

1. In a medium saucepan, combine grapefruit zest, grapefruit juice and syrup; cook over low heat for 10 minutes. Stir in basil, remove from heat and let stand for 30 minutes. Transfer to a bowl. Cover and refrigerate until completely cold or overnight.

2. Stir juice mixture. Transfer to an ice cream maker and churn until just soft and slushy-smooth, not firm. Serve in chilled glasses.

✿ Variation

Though basil works beautifully with grapefruit, we also like tarragon or rosemary. The collaboration between grapefruit juice and these herbs is a winning one.

Pink Grapefruit Star Anise Ice

SERVES 8 TO 10

Think pink for a wonderfully refreshing ice that's a perfect palate refresher or a welcome dessert. The star anise gives it an exotic edge.

Tip: To get the required fresh grapefruit juice, you'll need 3 to 4 pink grapefruits, seeds removed.

Serve this ice in champagne flutes, topped with a few raspberries and chopped fresh mint.

2 cups	water	500 mL
1⅓ cups	granulated sugar	325 mL
3	whole star anise	3
4 cups	freshly squeezed pink grapefruit juice (see Tips, left)	1 L

1. In a medium saucepan, bring water, sugar and star anise to a boil. Cook, stirring, until sugar is dissolved. Remove from heat and let stand for 15 minutes. Discard star anise. Let cool.

2. Stir juice into sugar mixture. Transfer to a clean large bowl. Cover and refrigerate until completely cold or overnight.

3. Stir juice mixture. Transfer to an ice cream maker and freeze according to manufacturer's instructions.

Lime Granita

More sour than sweet, this granita is incredibly refreshing on a hot summer day. A little bit of it is also excellent as a between-courses palate cleanser.

- 13- by 9-inch (3 L) metal baking pan

2 cups	water	500 mL
1 cup	granulated sugar	250 mL
	Zest of 1 lime	
1 cup	freshly squeezed lime juice	250 mL

1. In a bowl, stir together water, sugar, lime zest and juice until sugar is dissolved.

2. Pour into baking pan and freeze for 1 hour or until ice forms at the edges of the pan.

3. Using a fork, break up ice and stir to distribute frozen portions evenly. Freeze for 30 minutes or until solid.

4. Using a fork, stir to break up ice crystals. Continue freezing, stirring the mixture every 20 minutes, until slushy.

Cantaloupe Ice

SERVES 6 TO 8

This works best with very ripe cantaloupe, but you can also use honeydew melon. If you want to pair melon with another fruit, blueberry works particularly well; just add 1/2 cup (125 mL) fresh blueberries to the food processor along with the melon.

1	large ripe cantaloupe, peeled, seeded and chopped (about 8 cups/2 L)	1
1 cup	Simple Syrup (see recipe, page 20)	250 mL
1/4 cup	orange juice	50 mL
1/4 cup	freshly squeezed lemon juice	50 mL

1. In a food processor or blender, purée cantaloupe, syrup, orange juice and lemon juice until smooth. Transfer to a bowl. Cover and refrigerate until completely cold or overnight.

2. Stir cantaloupe mixture. Transfer to an ice cream maker and freeze according to manufacturer's instructions.

Spicy Honeydew Granita

Cinnamon and nutmeg give this honeydew ice an exotic twist.

Tip: If the granita becomes solid, use a food processor to break the chunks into smaller pieces before serving.

- 13- by 9-inch (3 L) metal baking pan

3 cups	honeydew melon chunks	750 mL
½ cup	Simple Syrup (see recipe, page 20)	125 mL
2 tbsp	freshly squeezed lime juice	25 mL
¼ tsp	ground cinnamon	1 mL
¼ tsp	ground nutmeg	1 mL

1. In a food processor or blender, purée melon, syrup, lime juice, cinnamon and nutmeg until smooth.

2. Pour into baking pan and freeze for about 1 hour or until ice forms at the edges of the pan.

3. Using a fork, break up ice and stir to distribute frozen portions evenly. Freeze for 30 minutes or until solid.

4. Using a fork, stir to break up ice crystals. Continue freezing, stirring the mixture every 20 minutes, until slushy.

Watermelon Lemonade Ice

Scrape this frozen ice into a slushie on a hot day. Or try it frozen solid in ice-pop molds (see Tip, below).

Tip: To make ice pops, divide mixture among 8 ice-pop molds. Cover and freeze until firm.

- 13- by 9-inch (3 L) metal baking pan

2 cups	finely chopped seeded watermelon	500 mL
1 cup	frozen lemonade concentrate, thawed	250 mL

1. In a food processor or blender, purée watermelon with lemonade concentrate until smooth.

2. Pour into baking pan and freeze for 1 hour or until ice forms at the edges of the pan.

3. Using a fork, break up ice and stir to distribute frozen portions evenly. Freeze for 30 minutes or until solid.

Watermelon Mint Ice

You can make this with red or yellow watermelon. The addition of orange and lime juices gives the recipe an even-more-tropical flavor. You can also serve this when it's slushy, just before it freezes, for a treat that kids especially will love!

Tip: When using herbs, make sure they have not been treated with pesticides. Treat herbs to a light wash in soapy water and rinse very well.

2 cups	chopped seeded watermelon	500 mL
1 cup	Simple Syrup (see recipe, page 20)	250 mL
½ cup	orange juice	125 mL
1 tbsp	freshly squeezed lime juice	15 mL
1 tbsp	finely chopped fresh mint (see Tip, left)	15 mL

1. In a food processor or blender, purée watermelon, syrup, orange juice, lime juice and mint until smooth. Transfer to a bowl. Cover and refrigerate until completely cold or overnight.

2. Stir fruit mixture. Transfer to an ice cream maker and freeze according to manufacturer's instructions.

Mexican Watermelon Granita

This is our take on paletas, Mexican Popsicles that combine unusual flavors; if this is too hot for your taste, decrease the amount of cayenne pepper. To expand on the Mexican theme, serve the granita with a splash of tequila on top.

Tips: If the granita becomes solid, use a food processor to break the chunks into smaller pieces before serving.

If you prefer a smoother texture, the purée can be frozen in an ice cream maker.

- 13- by 9-inch (3 L) metal baking pan

3 cups	seeded watermelon chunks	750 mL
¼ cup	granulated sugar	50 mL
1 tbsp	freshly squeezed lemon juice	15 mL
¼ tsp	cayenne pepper	1 mL

1. In a food processor or blender, purée watermelon, sugar, lemon juice and cayenne until smooth.

2. Pour into baking pan and freeze for about 1 hour or until ice forms at the edges of the pan.

3. Using a fork, break up ice and stir to distribute frozen portions evenly. Freeze for 30 minutes or until solid.

4. Using a fork, stir to break up ice crystals. Continue freezing, stirring the mixture every 20 minutes, until slushy.

Watermelon Frozen Margaritas

We call this updated cocktail of the '90s The Adult Slushy. With this much liquor in it, it won't freeze completely, so it's best enjoyed in slush form straight from the ice cream maker.

Tip: You can decrease the Simple Syrup to ¼ cup (50 mL) if you prefer your margaritas less sweet.

Serving suggestion: Rub the rim of a glass with lime, then dip in salt. Fill with slushy Watermelon Frozen Margarita and serve with a thick straw.

5 cups	chopped seeded watermelon	1.25 L
½ cup	Simple Syrup (see recipe, page 20)	125 mL
½ cup	freshly squeezed lime juice	125 mL
¾ cup	white tequila	175 mL

1. In a food processor or blender, purée watermelon, syrup and lime juice until smooth. Transfer to a bowl. Stir in tequila. Cover and refrigerate until completely cold or overnight.

2. Stir fruit mixture. Transfer to an ice cream maker and freeze according to manufacturer's instructions.

Variation

Frozen Watermelon Mojitos: Substitute dark rum for the tequila. Add 2 tbsp (25 mL) chopped fresh mint.

Apricot Ice with Cumin and Chipotle Pepper

This easy dessert offers a little exotica and can be served as a palate cleanser between courses, on its own, or with something chocolatey.

½ cup	Simple Syrup (see recipe, page 20)	125 mL
1	can (14 oz/398 mL) apricot halves in light syrup	1
1 tsp	ground cumin	5 mL
¼ tsp	crushed dried chipotle pepper or chili pepper	1 mL

1. In a food processor or blender, purée syrup, apricots with syrup, cumin and chipotle pepper until smooth. Transfer to a bowl. Cover and refrigerate until completely cold or overnight.

2. Stir apricot mixture. Transfer to an ice cream maker and freeze according to manufacturer's instructions.

Peach and Plum Slushy

SERVES 8

In this recipe, the intense flavors of fresh late-summer fruits are enjoyed without the richness of dairy. Serve with biscotti for dipping.

Tip: If you want a very smooth purée, press it through a fine sieve.

2 cups	chopped peeled peaches	500 mL
2 cups	chopped purple prune plums	500 mL
½ cup	granulated sugar	125 mL
½ cup	prune juice	125 mL
1 tbsp	chopped fresh rosemary	15 mL

1. In a medium saucepan, combine peaches, plums, sugar, prune juice and rosemary; cover and cook over low heat for about 20 minutes or until fruit is very soft.

2. Transfer to a food processor and purée until smooth. Transfer to a bowl. Let cool to room temperature. Cover and refrigerate until completely cold or overnight.

3. Stir fruit mixture. Transfer to an ice cream maker and churn until just soft and slushy-smooth, not firm. Serve in chilled glasses.

Variation
Substitute mango juice, white grape juice or even water for the prune juice.

Plum and Cabernet Ice with Black Pepper

SERVES 8

Though this is technically an ice, in that it contains no dairy, it has the appearance of a light ice cream. Expect a substantial kick from the black pepper; for less heat, reduce the amount of peppercorns.

2 cups	chopped red or black plums	500 mL
¾ cup	granulated sugar	175 mL
¾ cup	Cabernet Sauvignon or other dry red wine	175 mL
¾ cup	water	175 mL
	Grated zest of ½ lemon	
1 tsp	whole black peppercorns	5 mL

1. In a medium, heavy saucepan, combine plums, sugar, wine, water, lemon zest and peppercorns; bring to a boil. Reduce heat to low and simmer for 20 minutes or until fruit is very soft. Remove from heat and let cool to room temperature.

2. Using the back of a wooden spoon, press through a fine sieve into a bowl. Cover and refrigerate until completely cold or overnight.

3. Stir fruit mixture. Transfer to an ice cream maker and freeze according to manufacturer's instructions.

Mango Ginger Ice

1 cup	Simple Syrup (see recipe, page 20)	250 mL
1	large ripe banana, sliced	1
2	cans (each 14 oz/398 mL) mango in syrup	2
1 tsp	grated gingerroot	5 mL

1. In a food processor or blender, purée syrup, banana, mango with syrup and ginger until smooth. Transfer to a bowl. Cover and refrigerate until completely cold or overnight.

2. Stir mango mixture. Transfer to an ice cream maker and freeze according to manufacturer's instructions.

Mango Basics

The mango is a versatile fruit that is equally at home in sorbets and salsas, ice creams and chutneys. It is low in calories and high in fiber, and it has plenty of beta carotene, which the body converts to vitamin A.

Kiwi and Candied Ginger Sorbet

This dessert has the smoothness of a sorbet but is really a fruit ice — and a sophisticated, delicious one at that.

Tip: This recipe contains a raw egg white. If the food safety of raw eggs is a concern for you, use the pasteurized liquid egg white instead.

½ cup	granulated sugar	125 mL
¼ cup	water	50 mL
6	kiwifruits, peeled and chopped (about 2 cups/500 mL)	6
¼ cup	finely chopped candied ginger	50 mL
1 tbsp	freshly squeezed lime juice	15 mL
1	egg white, lightly beaten, or 2 tbsp (25 mL) pasteurized liquid egg white	1

1. In a medium, heavy saucepan, bring sugar and water to a boil, stirring to dissolve sugar. Set aside.

2. In a food processor, purée kiwifruits, ginger, lime juice and sugar syrup until smooth. Transfer to a bowl. Cover and refrigerate until completely cold or overnight.

3. Stir kiwi mixture. Transfer to an ice cream maker and churn until thick. Add egg white and finish freezing according to manufacturer's instructions.

Kiwi Banana Lime Ice

2 cups	Simple Syrup (see recipe, page 20)	500 mL
6	kiwifruits, peeled and chopped (about 2 cups/500 mL)	6
1	large banana, sliced	1
1 tbsp	freshly squeezed lime juice	15 mL

1. In a food processor or blender, purée syrup, kiwifruits, banana and lime juice until smooth. Transfer to a bowl. Cover and refrigerate until completely cold or overnight.

2. Stir fruit mixture. Transfer to an ice cream maker and freeze according to manufacturer's instructions.

✺ Variation

Mellow Yellow Kiwi Banana Lime Ice: Instead of green kiwifruits, use the golden kiwifruits increasingly found in North American markets.

Lychee Ice

Even if you'd never think of peeling your own fresh lychees, you'll love this exotic ice. Instead of fresh fruit, it's made with lychees canned in syrup that are available in most supermarkets or any Asian grocery store. For an extra-special twist, add ½ cup (125 mL) chopped crystallized ginger in the last 5 minutes of freezing. Or serve as is with the chopped ginger on top.

Tip: Lychee Ice is a delicious and proper ending to a meal celebrating Chinese New Year. Lychees are one of the "lucky" fruits given to bring in the new year! Fresh unpeeled lychees, sold in Asian supermarkets, can be piled high in glass bowls or jars as festive table decorations.

1	can (19 oz/540 mL) lychees in syrup	1
1 cup	apple juice	250 mL
1 tbsp	freshly squeezed lime juice	15 mL

1. In a food processor or blender, purée lychees with syrup until smooth.

2. Transfer to a bowl. Stir in apple juice and lime juice. Cover and refrigerate until completely cold or overnight.

3. Stir lychee mixture. Transfer to an ice cream maker and freeze according to manufacturer's instructions.

Papaya Ice

Make sure you use only the ripest papayas for this refreshing recipe, which has the consistency of ice cream, thanks to the addition of a banana. This is a terrific dessert for a hot, steamy day. Serve with crisp shortbreads or gingersnaps on the side.

2 cups	chopped ripe papaya	500 mL
1 cup	Simple Syrup (see recipe, page 20)	250 mL
1	large ripe banana, sliced	1
	Juice of 2 limes	

1. In a food processor or blender, purée papaya, syrup, banana and lime juice until smooth. Transfer to a bowl. Cover and refrigerate until completely cold or overnight.

2. Stir papaya mixture. Transfer to an ice cream maker and freeze according to manufacturer's instructions.

✿ Variation

You can develop your own version by playing with flavors and combinations. For example, instead of 2 cups (500 mL) chopped papaya, try 1 cup (250 mL) chopped papaya and 1 cup (250 mL) chopped mango.

Passion Fruit and Pear Ice

The addition of Pernod, an anise-flavored liqueur, makes this a perfect between-courses palate cleanser for a sophisticated dinner party. Without the liquor, it's a tasty and smooth ice that pairs well with something chocolatey — even the simplest fudge brownie.

1 cup	passion fruit juice	250 mL
1	can (14 oz/398 mL) pears in light syrup	1
½	sliced banana	½
1 tbsp	Pernod (optional)	15 mL

1. In a food processor or blender, purée passion fruit juice, pears with syrup, banana and Pernod (if using) until smooth. Transfer to a bowl. Cover and refrigerate until completely cold or overnight.

2. Stir fruit mixture. Transfer to an ice cream maker and freeze according to manufacturer's instructions.

Passion Fruit Basics

Fresh passion fruit is the size of an egg. Its purple skin starts out smooth, but it is not considered ripe and ready to eat until the skin wrinkles. Spoon out the flesh and eat the seeds. In the above recipe, you can substitute 1 cup (250 mL) of the flesh (with seeds) for the juice.

Pineapple Rum Ice

This ice is perfect for a Caribbean-themed party where you serve jerk chicken and black beans and rice.

2 cups	fresh pineapple chunks	500 mL
1 cup	Simple Syrup (see recipe, page 20)	250 mL
½	large ripe banana, sliced	½
1 tbsp	dark rum	15 mL

1. In a food processor or blender, purée pineapple, syrup, banana and rum until smooth. Transfer to a bowl. Cover and refrigerate until completely cold or overnight.

2. Stir fruit mixture. Transfer to an ice cream maker and freeze according to manufacturer's instructions.

Variation

Pineapple Maraschino Cherry Ice: Omit the rum. Add ½ cup (125 mL) drained roughly chopped maraschino cherries to the ice cream maker in the last 5 minutes of freezing and let the machine stir them in.

Pineapple Star Anise Ice

Truly exotic is the licorice-like taste of pretty star-shaped anise pods, which are popular in Chinese cooking. Serve with grilled or roasted pineapple slices or over old-fashioned pineapple upside-down cake.

1 cup	Simple Syrup (see recipe, page 20)	250 mL
4	whole star anise	4
2 cups	fresh pineapple chunks	500 mL
1 tbsp	freshly squeezed lemon juice	15 mL

1. In a medium saucepan, bring syrup and star anise to a boil. Reduce heat and simmer for 5 minutes. Let cool to room temperature. Discard star anise.

2. In a food processor or blender, purée syrup mixture, pineapple and lemon juice until smooth. Transfer to a bowl. Cover and refrigerate until completely cold or overnight.

3. Stir pineapple mixture. Transfer to an ice cream maker and freeze according to manufacturer's instructions.

Pomegranate Ice

Chock-full of antioxidants, simple to make and delicious, this ice is simply the best! For added glamor, sprinkle with pomegranate seeds and serve with your favorite biscotti.

Tips: If you're serving this as a palate cleanser, increase the lime juice to make it a little more tart.

Pomegranate seeds make a wonderful garnish for everything from couscous to lamb. One of our favorite tricks is to fill ice cube trays with pomegranate seeds and juice; pomegranate ice cubes add a special touch to lemonade, beer, and gin and tonic.

2 cups	unsweetened pure pomegranate juice	500 mL
1 cup	Simple Syrup (see recipe, page 20)	250 mL
2 tbsp	freshly squeezed lime juice	25 mL

1. In a bowl, combine pomegranate juice, syrup and lime juice. Cover and refrigerate until completely cold or overnight.

2. Stir juice mixture. Transfer to an ice cream maker and freeze according to manufacturer's instructions.

Variation
Pomegranate Orange Ice: Replace 1/2 cup (125 mL) of the pomegranate juice with 1/2 cup (125 mL) freshly squeezed orange juice.

Almond Milk and Thyme Ice

SERVES 8 TO 10

If you're allergic to eggs or want a frozen dessert that's not too rich, this ice is perfect. Straining out the ground almonds (rather than freezing them in the milk) gives this a smoother texture.

4 cups	milk	1 L
½ cup	liquid honey	125 mL
⅔ cup	ground blanched almonds	150 mL
½ tsp	almond extract	2 mL
1 tbsp	chopped fresh thyme	15 mL

1. In a medium saucepan over low heat, cook milk and honey, stirring, until honey is dissolved. Remove from heat and stir in almonds, almond extract and thyme. Let steep for 20 minutes.

2. Using the back of a wooden spoon, press through a fine sieve into a bowl. Cover and refrigerate until completely cold or overnight.

3. Stir almond milk mixture. Transfer to an ice cream maker and freeze according to manufacturer's instructions.

Almond Snow

2 cups	filtered water	500 mL
1/2 cup	marzipan (almond paste)	125 mL
1 tsp	double-intensity vanilla	5 mL

What an amazing transformation! Marzipan blended with water at high speed turns white and has the consistency of a creamy gelato. Use any leftover marzipan to form tiny decorative fruits, which you and your kids can paint with food coloring.

Tip: Marzipan, a sugary almond paste, can be purchased at gourmet stores, as can double-intensity vanilla.

1. In a food processor or blender, purée water, marzipan and vanilla until smooth.

2. Using the back of a wooden spoon, press through a fine sieve into a bowl. Cover and refrigerate until completely cold or overnight.

3. Stir marzipan mixture. Transfer to an ice cream maker and freeze according to manufacturer's instructions.

Coffee Granita

This is the classic Italian slushy, usually served in a tall glass and topped with whipped cream. Granitas are frozen desserts made in the freezer by hand, not in an ice cream machine. It seems daunting but is really easy to do and worth the extra bit of work.

- 13- by 9-inch (3 L) metal baking pan

4 cups	freshly brewed strong coffee	1 L
1 cup	granulated sugar	250 mL
	Zest of 1 lemon	
1 tsp	vanilla	5 mL
2	whole star anise	2

1. In a bowl, stir together coffee, sugar, lemon zest, vanilla and star anise until sugar is dissolved. Let cool to room temperature.

2. Discard star anise. Pour mixture into baking pan. Freeze for about 1 hour or until ice forms at the edges of the pan.

3. Using a fork, break up ice and stir to distribute frozen portions evenly. Freeze for 30 minutes or until solid.

4. Using a fork, stir to break up ice crystals. Continue freezing, stirring the mixture every 20 minutes, until slushy. Serve with whipped cream.

Spiced Wine Sorbet

Anyone who loves mulled wine will enjoy it in frozen form. We like to serve it with honeyed oranges on the side as a heady finish to a dinner of roast lamb.

Tip: Even though you reduce the liquid, and thereby cook off much of the alcohol, we found that this sorbet doesn't freeze as well as some. This doesn't detract from its enjoyment though. It's a winner, for sure!

1	bottle (750 mL) dry red wine	1
1 cup	granulated sugar	250 mL
1 cup	apple juice	250 mL
1	lemon, sliced	1
1	orange, sliced	1
3	cinnamon sticks, broken in half	3
10	whole cloves	10
10	whole black peppercorns	10
1/2 tsp	ground allspice	2 mL

1. In a large saucepan, bring all the ingredients to a boil. Reduce heat to medium and cook until reduced by one-third, about 15 minutes. Remove from heat and let cool.

2. Strain into a clean large bowl. Cover and refrigerate until completely cold or overnight.

3. Stir wine mixture. Transfer to an ice cream maker and freeze according to manufacturer's instructions.

Cuban Ice

This is our version of the mojito, the classic Cuban cocktail. Serve it as a starter, a palate cleanser or a light dessert for a Latin-themed dinner.

Tip: When using herbs, make sure they have not been treated with pesticides. Treat herbs to a light wash in soapy water and rinse very well.

2 cups	Simple Syrup (see recipe, page 20)	500 mL
	Juice of 2 limes	
½ cup	white rum	125 mL
¼ cup	chopped fresh mint (see Tip, left)	50 mL

1. In a bowl, stir together syrup, lime juice and rum. Cover and refrigerate until completely cold or overnight.

2. Stir syrup mixture. Transfer to an ice cream maker and freeze according to manufacturer's instructions. Garnish each serving with mint.

Beet Apple Slush

2 cups	beet juice	500 mL
1 cup	apple juice	250 mL
¼ cup	granulated sugar	50 mL

Beets would seem an unlikely choice for a palate cleanser, but this delicious, simple recipe is refreshing between courses or as a summertime starter. You can use freshly squeezed beet juice or bottled — either will work fine. A word to the wise: where there are beets, there are bound to be stains.

1. In a bowl, stir together beet juice, apple juice and sugar until sugar is dissolved. Cover and refrigerate until completely cold or overnight.

2. Stir juice mixture. Transfer to an ice cream maker and freeze according to manufacturer's instructions.

Beet Basics

Beets are a source of folate, fiber and potassium, so this is one treat your body will thank you for.

Tip: Enjoy Beet Apple Slush as a marvelous summer afternoon cooler in place of ice cream. You can omit the sugar, or decrease the amount to taste, if you prefer.

Serving suggestion: Garnish with a dollop of sweetened sour cream and chopped fresh mint.

Carrot Ice

Save those carrot sticks for lunch boxes and try serving this as a palate cleanser at an adult party. Or, topped with chopped crystallized ginger, serve it as a memorable and fine finish to a more formal occasion. You can purchase carrot juice at health-food stores or you can make your own with a juicer.

Tip: If you're serving vegetable-based ices between courses as a palate cleanser, a little is all that's required. Instead of the big scoop traditionally offered, try serving small tastes in demitasse cups or in stand-alone porcelain Chinese spoons.

3 cups	carrot juice	750 mL
1	small carrot, grated	1
½ cup	Simple Syrup (see recipe, page 20)	125 mL
¼ cup	apple juice	50 mL
1 tsp	grated lemon zest	5 mL
1 tbsp	freshly squeezed lemon juice	25 mL

1. In a bowl, stir together carrot juice, carrot, syrup, apple juice and lemon zest and juice until combined. Cover and refrigerate until completely cold or overnight.

2. Stir carrot mixture. Transfer to an ice cream maker and freeze according to manufacturer's instructions.

❧ Variation
Carrot Cranberry Ice: Replace 1 cup (250 mL) of the carrot juice with 1 cup (250 mL) cranberry juice.

Cucumber Ice

SERVES 8 TO 10

As a summer dinner starter, this has several possibilities. Serve it drizzled with yogurt, paired with Tomato Basil Ice (see recipe, page 228) or surrounded by baby shrimp.

Serving suggestion:
When serving a trio of ices, consider a full range of flavors and include a vegetable-based ice, such as this one, along with two citrus ices, say mandarin orange and pink grapefruit with star anise.

2	large English cucumbers, peeled and roughly chopped (about 4 cups/1 L)	2
2 cups	Simple Syrup (see recipe, page 20)	500 mL
1/4 cup	chopped fresh dill	50 mL
1/4 tsp	salt	1 mL
Dash	hot pepper sauce	Dash

1. In a food processor or blender, purée cucumbers, syrup, dill, salt and hot pepper sauce until smooth. Transfer to a bowl. Cover and refrigerate until completely cold or overnight.

2. Stir cucumber mixture. Transfer to an ice cream maker and freeze according to manufacturer's instructions.

Variation
Cucumber pairs well with several different herbs. Try substituting chopped fresh mint or thyme for the dill in this recipe.

Tomato Basil Ice

This ice is a welcome first course during a heat wave. Serve it on its own or dollop it in chilled corn or cucumber soup. For the best flavor, wait until tomatoes are at their ripest.

Tip: When using herbs, make sure they have not been treated with pesticides. Treat herbs to a light wash in soapy water and rinse very well.

5	large ripe tomatoes (about 3 lbs/1.5 kg)	5
½ cup	tomato juice	125 mL
¼ cup	chopped fresh basil leaves (see Tip, left)	50 mL
¼ cup	freshly squeezed lemon juice	50 mL
2 tbsp	tomato paste	25 mL
1 tbsp	olive oil	15 mL
	Salt and freshly ground black pepper	

1. Peel, core and seed tomatoes. Chop.

2. In a food processor or blender, purée tomatoes, tomato juice, basil, lemon juice, tomato paste and oil until smooth. Transfer to a bowl. Add salt and pepper to taste. Cover and refrigerate until completely cold or overnight.

3. Stir tomato mixture. Transfer to an ice cream maker and freeze according to manufacturer's instructions.

Drinks & Ice Pops

Banana Mango Batidas

SERVES 6

A friend of ours raved about batidas, the fruity blended drinks she tasted throughout Latin America. They are often used as a cocktail base (you can add 1/4 cup/ 50 mL light rum to this recipe, if you wish.) But we like to transform them from smoothies to slushies and serve them in chilled glasses rimmed with lime and brown sugar.

1	ripe banana, chopped into small chunks	1
1 cup	chopped peeled ripe mango	250 mL
1 cup	milk	250 mL
1/4 cup	freshly squeezed lime juice	50 mL
1 tbsp	granulated sugar	15 mL
3 cups	ice cubes	750 mL

1. In a food processor or blender, purée banana, mango, milk, lime juice, sugar and ice until smooth, about 1 minute. Transfer to a bowl. Cover and refrigerate until completely cold or overnight.

2. Stir fruit mixture. Transfer to an ice cream maker and freeze according to manufacturer's instructions until semifrozen and slushy. Serve immediately.

Lemony Float

This summer treat is a good way to get your ice cream fix without wrestling with a messy cone. It's perfect for long, slow sipping by a cool northern lake.

| 2 cups | cold lemonade | 250 mL |
| 2 | large scoops ice cream, such as Old-Fashioned Vanilla Ice Cream (see recipe, page 40), Pucker-Up Ice Cream (see recipe, page 87) or Ginger Ice Cream (see recipe, page 57) Chopped fresh mint leaves | 2 |

1. Pour lemonade into two tall glasses. Add one scoop of ice cream to each glass.

2. Garnish with mint.

Variation

Lemon-Lime Soda Float: Use your favorite lemon-lime soda pop instead of lemonade. Garnish with fresh lime slices instead of, or in addition to, mint.

Gin Fizz

Gin and tonic is a popular happy-hour standby. This fruity version, meant to be eaten as well as sipped, is a welcome alternative as a late-afternoon adult pick-me-up.

Serving suggestion:
Rim each glass with lemon, then dip in sugar.

1 cup	mixed berries, fresh or frozen	250 mL
1 tbsp	lemon zest	15 mL
¼ cup	freshly squeezed lemon juice	50 mL
4	scoops Lime Granita (see recipe, page 201)	4
½ cup	gin	125 mL
1 cup	tonic water	250 mL

1. In a bowl, toss together berries and lemon zest and juice.

2. Divide berry mixture among four tall glasses. Add one scoop Lime Granita to each.

3. Divide gin among glasses. Top with tonic water.

Coffee Frappé

Ice-blended creamy coffee beverages are sweeping the country. Here's our version to be served in coffee cups. A splash of coffee liqueur over each serving is optional.

Tip: Use your favorite flavored coffee in place of the espresso to create your own signature Coffee Frappé.

8	scoops coffee ice cream, such as Café au Lait Ice Cream (see recipe, page 122)	8
2 cups	crushed ice	500 mL
1 cup	cold espresso	250 mL
	Ground cinnamon to taste	

1. In a food processor or blender, purée half of the coffee ice cream, the ice and espresso until smooth.

2. Pour into four cups or glasses. Top each with one scoop of the remaining ice cream and sprinkle with cinnamon.

Variations

Coffee Butterscotch Frappé: Add ¼ cup (50 mL) butterscotch sauce with the espresso. Top with a drizzle of butterscotch sauce rather than ground cinnamon.

Almond Coffee Frappé: Add 1 tbsp (15 mL) almond extract with the espresso.

Mocha Frappé: Add ¼ cup (50 mL) chocolate syrup with the espresso. Top with a drizzle of chocolate syrup rather than ground cinnamon.

Coffee Frappé with Black Pepper: Top each serving with a sprinkling of freshly ground pepper.

Hot Chocolate with Cold Center

This is a perfect treat to enjoy on a chilly autumn afternoon after a few hours of yardwork. If you prefer, substitute your favorite powdered hot chocolate mix for the grated semisweet chocolate topping.

Tip: Use chocolate milk in place of the skim milk for a more chocolatey version.

2 cups	skim milk	500 mL
6 oz	semisweet chocolate, chopped	175 g
4	scoops chocolate ice cream	4
	Grated semisweet chocolate	

1. In a medium saucepan over medium heat, heat milk with chopped chocolate, stirring, until chocolate is melted and mixture is smooth and steaming.

2. Divide ice cream among four mugs. Pour milk mixture over top. Top with grated chocolate.

❧ Variation

Decadent Cow: Substitute chopped white chocolate for the semisweet chocolate. Top with grated white chocolate.

Raspberry Yogurt Ice Pops

SERVES 2 OR 3

Not only is this a healthy summer snack, but it's also one that kids (and adults) are sure to love. You can use your favorite fresh berries in this. We love the taste of raspberries despite their seeds.

- Ice-pop molds
- Popsicle sticks

2 cups	fresh raspberries	500 mL
1 cup	raspberry-flavored yogurt	250 mL
½ cup	water	125 mL
¼ cup	liquid honey	50 mL
1 tsp	lemon zest	5 mL

1. In a food processor or blender, purée raspberries. (If desired, press the raspberry purée through a sieve into a bowl to remove seeds.)

2. In a bowl, combine raspberry purée with yogurt. Mix well. Stir in water, honey and lemon zest.

3. Divide among ice-pop molds and freeze until slushy. Insert sticks. Return to freezer and freeze until firm.

❧ Variations

Peach Yogurt Ice Pops: Substitute 2 cups (500 mL) chopped pitted peeled peaches for the raspberries, and peach-flavored yogurt for the raspberry-flavored yogurt.

Kiwi Yogurt Ice Pops: Substitute 2 cups (500 mL) chopped peeled kiwifruits for the raspberries, and plain yogurt for the raspberry-flavored yogurt.

Cocktail Pops

SERVES 6

Who says finger foods always have to be savory? These one-bite ice creams are a great way to add a memorable moment to any party. The more flavorful the ice cream, the better: choose Pumpkin Ice Cream (page 136), Pucker-Up Ice Cream (page 87), Ginger Ice Cream (page 57) or Chocolate Mousse Ice Cream (page 25) — or make a variety of flavors so guests can choose.

Tip: To unmold, immerse the bottom of the ice cube tray in warm water for 30 seconds.

• Large ice cube tray

Assorted ice cream flavors
Popsicle sticks, lemongrass spears
or cinnamon sticks

1. Press ice cream into ice cube molds. Insert sticks.

2. Freeze until firm.

3. Unmold just before serving.

Lemon Martini Ice Pops

Plastic ice-pop molds are easy to find in the supermarket and are inexpensive, so you can experiment well beyond the traditional lemonade or orange juice pops. We especially like this adult martini version. Because of its liquid consistency, we recommend waiting until the mixture is semifrozen before inserting the sticks.

- Ice-pop mold
- Popsicle sticks

1½ cups	water	375 mL
¼ cup	granulated sugar	50 mL
	Zest of 1 lemon	
¼ cup	gin	50 mL
3 tbsp	dry vermouth	45 mL

1. In a medium saucepan over medium heat, heat water with sugar, stirring, until sugar is dissolved. Let cool to room temperature.

2. Transfer to a bowl. Stir in lemon zest, gin and vermouth. Cover and refrigerate until completely cold or overnight.

3. Stir syrup mixture. Pour into ice-pop molds and freeze until slushy. Insert sticks. Return to freezer and freeze until firm.

❧ Variation

Crantini Ice Pops: Substitute 1¾ cups (425 mL) cranberry juice for water and sugar. Add lemon, gin and vermouth and freeze as directed.

Pupsicles

MAKES 12 TO 16 TREATS

Because our dogs were eating yogurt from the time they were puppies, we decided to make a frozen treat just for them. Dogs are usually lactose intolerant, but as yogurt contains little lactose, they'll love this down to the last lick.

Tip: If you prefer, you can freeze this mixture in an ice cream maker.

- Large ice cube tray

1	ripe banana	1
1 cup	plain yogurt	250 mL
3 tbsp	creamy peanut butter	45 mL
2 tbsp	liquid honey	25 mL

1. In a food processor or blender, purée banana, yogurt, peanut butter and honey until smooth.

2. Pour into ice cube trays and freeze for individual treats.

Low-Fat Ice Milks, Yogurts & Non-Dairy Desserts

Vanilla Ice Milk

If you long for the taste of ice cream yet want to cut the fat, this ice milk gives you full value in the calcium and taste departments. Because of its lack of fat, ice milk tends to freeze rock-solid, so make sure you transfer it to the refrigerator for 15 minutes before serving. For added flavor, double the amount of pure vanilla extract. You can substitute low-fat chocolate milk for the skim milk for another taste treat.

2 cups	skim milk	500 mL
½ cup	granulated sugar	125 mL
6 tbsp	powdered dried non-fat milk	90 mL
1 ½ tsp	vanilla	7 mL

1. In a medium saucepan over low heat, stir together milk, sugar and powdered milk until the sugar and powdered milk are dissolved.

2. Stir in vanilla. Transfer to a bowl. Let cool to room temperature. Cover and refrigerate until completely cold or overnight.

3. Stir milk mixture. Transfer to an ice cream maker and freeze according to manufacturer's instructions.

Peach Yogurt Ice Pops and Kiwi Yogurt
Ice Pops (see Variations, page 235)

Mango Ginger Coulis (page 261)
and Hot Butterscotch Sauce (page 254)

Raspberry Buttermilk
Ice Cream (page 241)

Raspberry Buttermilk Ice Cream

SERVES 2 TO 3

Despite its name, buttermilk is lower in fat than cream or even whole milk. But the incredible creamy taste of this frozen concoction will have you trying buttermilk with other partners, such as strawberries or peaches. Just substitute the same amount of your favorite fresh fruit for the amount of berries called for here. Strain the raspberries through a sieve just before freezing if you want to eliminate the seeds.

1 cup	fresh raspberries, or frozen, drained of syrup	250 mL
1 cup	buttermilk	250 mL
3/4 cup	Simple Syrup (see recipe, page 20)	175 mL
1	large ripe banana, sliced	1

1. In a food processor or blender, purée raspberries, buttermilk, syrup and banana until smooth. Transfer to a bowl. Cover and refrigerate until completely cold or overnight.

2. Stir fruit mixture. Transfer to an ice cream maker and freeze according to manufacturer's instructions.

Vanilla Frozen Yogurt

SERVES 4 TO 6

Yogurt lovers will find this low-fat dessert delicious on its own — though it can also be dressed up for a party with a side of fresh berries or puréed apricots spiked with brandy.

1 ½ cups	1% milk	375 mL
1 tsp	unflavored gelatin	5 mL
½ cup	granulated sugar	125 mL
1 tsp	vanilla	5 mL
1 ½ cups	plain low-fat yogurt	375 mL

1. In a small saucepan, combine milk with gelatin. Let stand for 1 minute or until gelatin is softened. Stir over low heat until gelatin is dissolved.

2. Stir in sugar and vanilla until sugar is dissolved. Transfer to a bowl. Let cool to room temperature. Cover and refrigerate until completely cold or overnight.

3. Stir in yogurt. Transfer to an ice cream maker and freeze according to manufacturer's instructions.

Chocolate Honey Low-Fat Frozen Yogurt

1	container (26 oz/750 g) plain non-fat yogurt	1
⅓ cup	liquid honey	75 mL
1 tbsp	finely chopped bittersweet chocolate	15 mL

1. In a bowl, stir together yogurt, honey and chocolate. Cover and refrigerate until completely cold or overnight.

2. Stir yogurt mixture. Transfer to an ice cream maker and freeze according to manufacturer's instructions.

❧ Variation

Espresso Chocolate Yogurt: Add 1 tsp (5 mL) instant espresso powder with the chocolate.

Breakfast Yogurt: Add 1 tbsp (15 mL) granola and 1 tsp (5 mL) plump raisins with the chocolate.

Honeyed Apricot and Grape Frozen Yogurt

You can use a low-fat yogurt for this recipe or omit the yogurt altogether to produce an apricot ice.

1	can (14 oz/398 mL) apricots in syrup	1
½ cup	white grape juice	125 mL
½ cup	liquid honey	125 mL
1 cup	plain yogurt	250 mL
1 tsp	fresh thyme leaves	5 mL

1. In a food processor or blender, purée apricots with syrup and grape juice until smooth.

2. Transfer to a bowl and stir in honey. Fold in yogurt and thyme. Cover and refrigerate until completely cold or overnight.

3. Stir apricot mixture. Transfer to an ice cream maker and freeze according to manufacturer's instructions.

Orange Frozen Yogurt

SERVES 4

*Try this for breakfast with
a side of sliced bananas
and strawberries.*

2	egg yolks	2
1/3 cup	packed brown sugar	75 mL
1/2 cup	2% milk	125 mL
1 1/4 cups	plain yogurt	300 mL
1 tbsp	orange zest	15 mL
1/4 cup	freshly squeezed orange juice	50 mL
1/4 cup	granola	50 mL

1. In a bowl, whisk egg yolks with sugar until thickened and pale yellow. Set aside.

2. In a medium saucepan over medium-low heat, heat milk until bubbles appear around the edge of pan. Gradually whisk into the egg mixture.

3. Return the entire mixture to the saucepan. Cook over low heat, stirring constantly, until the mixture is thick enough to coat the back of a wooden spoon. Be careful not to let it boil. Strain into a clean large bowl. Let cool to room temperature.

4. Cover and refrigerate until completely cold or overnight.

5. Stir in yogurt, orange zest and juice. Transfer to an ice cream maker and freeze according to manufacturer's instructions.

6. Serve sprinkled with granola.

Peach Frozen Yogurt

SERVES 4

In this recipe, the gelatin acts as a stabilizer. As peaches can have a mild taste depending on their variety and ripeness, we suggest adding chopped dried apricots to give the flavor some additional punch.

½ cup	granulated sugar	125 mL
½ cup	milk	125 mL
1 tsp	unflavored gelatin	5 mL
1 tbsp	corn syrup	15 mL
1 ½ lbs	peaches, peeled and sliced, about 6 small peaches	750 g
¼ cup	finely chopped dried apricots	50 mL
1 cup	plain yogurt	250 mL
¼ tsp	vanilla	1 mL

1. In a medium saucepan, stir together sugar, milk and gelatin. Let stand for 1 minute or until gelatin is softened.

2. Cook over low heat, stirring constantly, for 3 minutes or until gelatin is dissolved.

3. Transfer to a large bowl. Stir in corn syrup. Let cool to room temperature.

4. In a food processor or blender, purée peaches until smooth. Add apricots and pulse until smooth. Stir into milk mixture along with yogurt and vanilla. Cover and refrigerate until completely cold or overnight.

5. Stir peach mixture. Transfer to an ice cream maker and freeze according to manufacturer's instructions.

Peachy Maple Frozen Yogurt

SERVES 6

Here's an easy way to ensure that your family gets a healthy yet delicious breakfast.

Tip: If you don't have an ice cream maker, you can freeze this mixture in individual ice-pop molds for breakfast on the run.

2 cups	chopped peeled peaches	500 mL
2 cups	plain yogurt	500 mL
½ cup	pure maple syrup	125 mL

1. In a food processor or blender, purée peaches, yogurt and maple syrup until smooth. Transfer to a bowl. Cover and refrigerate until completely cold or overnight.

2. Stir peach mixture. Transfer to an ice cream maker and freeze according to manufacturer's instructions.

Variation
Substitute pitted sweet cherries for the peaches.

Banana Soy Freeze

Today's soy beverages taste much better than those of a decade ago. This banana soy "ice cream" is perfect for people who have dairy allergies or who just want to get more beneficial soy into their diet.

½ cup	Simple Syrup (see recipe, page 20)	125 mL
1 tbsp	freshly squeezed lemon juice	15 mL
2	large ripe bananas, sliced	2
1½ cups	vanilla-flavored soy beverage	375 mL
¼ tsp	vanilla	1 mL

1. In a food processor or blender, purée syrup, lemon juice and bananas until smooth.

2. Transfer to a large bowl. Stir in soy beverage and vanilla. Cover and refrigerate until completely cold or overnight.

3. Stir banana mixture. Transfer to an ice cream maker and freeze according to manufacturer's instructions.

Chocolate Soy "Ice Cream"

With so many soy beverages to choose from, you can easily make this mock ice cream at home. We used milk chocolate, but you can substitute shavings of your favorite bittersweet chocolate bar.

2 cups	chocolate-flavored soy beverage	500 mL
1 cup	Simple Syrup (see recipe, page 20)	250 mL
¼ cup	shaved milk chocolate	50 mL
1 tsp	vanilla	5 mL

1. In a bowl, stir together soy beverage, syrup, shaved chocolate and vanilla until combined. Cover and refrigerate until completely cold or overnight.

2. Stir soy mixture. Transfer to an ice cream maker and freeze according to manufacturer's instructions.

Fig and Tofu "Ice Cream"

This "ice cream" is completely dairy-free. It's tasty and healthy and has all the creaminess of the real thing.

1 cup	dried figs	250 mL
1 cup	apple juice	250 mL
1/2 cup	cubed drained semi-firm tofu	125 mL
2/3 cup	unsweetened plain soy beverage	150 mL
1/2 tsp	ground cinnamon	2 mL

1. In a medium saucepan over medium heat, bring figs and apple juice to a simmer. Cook for 10 minutes, stirring occasionally. Remove from heat and let stand for 1 hour or until figs are plump.

2. In a food processor or blender, purée fig mixture with tofu until smooth.

3. Transfer to a bowl. Stir in soy beverage and cinnamon. Cover and refrigerate until completely cold or overnight.

4. Stir soy mixture. Transfer to an ice cream maker and freeze according to manufacturer's instructions.

Sauces

Chocolate Espresso Sauce

**MAKES 1½ CUPS
(375 mL)**

This sauce is a perfect topping for chocolate, vanilla or coffee ice cream. The best part is that it lasts longer than your store-bought latte.

- Double boiler

1	package (8 oz/250 g) chocolate chips	1
1 cup	whipping (35%) cream	250 mL
1 tbsp	cold brewed espresso	15 mL

1. In the top half of a double boiler over simmering water, stir together chocolate chips, cream and espresso until chocolate is melted.

2. Let cool to room temperature.

3. Serve over your favorite ice cream. Be as creative as you like with combinations. Sauce will keep, covered and refrigerated, for up to 3 days.

Hot Fudge Sauce

**MAKES 3 CUPS
(750 mL)**

Nothing says "classic combo" more than vanilla ice cream with hot fudge sauce. Whether you pour it over sundae fixings or just a single scoop, this lick-your-finger sauce will become an instant favorite.

- Double boiler

4 oz	bittersweet chocolate, chopped	125 g
½ cup	butter	125 mL
¾ cup	unsweetened cocoa powder	175 mL
1½ cups	granulated sugar	375 mL
½ cup	milk	125 mL
½ cup	whipping (35%) cream	125 mL

1. In the top half of a double boiler over simmering water, melt chocolate with butter, stirring constantly. Whisk in cocoa powder until smooth.

2. In a separate saucepan, mix together sugar, milk and cream. Cook over low heat, whisking constantly, until sugar is dissolved. Add chocolate mixture and cook, stirring often, until completely smooth and thick enough to coat the back of a wooden spoon.

3. Serve hot over chocolate, vanilla or any berry ice cream. Sauce will keep, covered and refrigerated, for up to 1 week.

Hot Butterscotch Sauce

MAKES 2½ CUPS (625 mL)

This sauce is the classic butterscotch sundae sauce. It is so delectable, we guarantee you will enjoy it all immediately.

1 cup	packed brown sugar	250 mL
1 cup	corn syrup	250 mL
¼ cup	unsalted butter	50 mL
¼ tsp	salt	1 mL
¾ cup	whipping (35%) cream	175 mL

1. In a medium saucepan, combine brown sugar, corn syrup, butter and salt. Cook over low heat, stirring constantly, until sugar is dissolved.

2. Increase heat to medium-high and bring to a boil.

3. Remove from heat. Carefully stir in cream, averting your face and holding the pan away from you and stirring until the mixture is smooth and foaming subsides. Be careful not to let it spatter.

4. Serve warm over your favorite ice cream. For a killer combo, serve hot over Dulce de Leche Ice Cream (see recipe, page 48) or chocolate ice cream. Sauce will keep, covered and refrigerated, for up to 1 week.

Sticky Sauce

**MAKES 1 CUP
(250 mL)**

This is our version of the classic caramel sundae sauce. It's easy to whip up and elevates ice cream to a whole new level. It's so good, you'll be eating it straight from the pan.

½ cup	packed brown sugar	125 mL
⅓ cup	whipping (35%) cream	75 mL
¼ cup	butter	50 mL
1 tsp	vanilla	5 mL

1. In a medium saucepan, bring brown sugar, cream and butter to a boil, stirring, until smooth.

2. Reduce heat to low. Simmer for 5 minutes. Remove from heat. Stir in vanilla.

3. Serve hot or at room temperature as a topping for Classic Chocolate Ice Cream (see recipe, page 22) or drizzle over Baked Alaska (see recipe, page 41). Sauce will keep, covered and refrigerated, for up to 1 week.

Apple Brown Betty Sauce

**MAKES 3 CUPS
(750 mL)**

Granny Smith apples are our favorite for this recipe. We like it with Old-Fashioned Vanilla Ice Cream (see recipe, page 40) or Apple Brown Betty Ice Cream (see recipe, page 74).

2 tbsp	butter	25 mL
5	apples, peeled, cored and sliced	5
½ cup	packed brown sugar	125 mL
1 tbsp	ground cinnamon	15 mL
½ tsp	ground cloves	2 mL
½ tsp	ground nutmeg	2 mL

1. In a medium saucepan over low heat, melt butter. Add apples. Cook, stirring occasionally, for 4 minutes or until softened.

2. Stir in brown sugar, cinnamon, cloves and nutmeg. Cook, stirring often, for 5 minutes or until sugar is dissolved and apples are soft.

3. Serve hot or at room temperature over your favorite ice cream. Sauce will keep, covered and refrigerated, for up to 1 week.

Banana Caramel Sauce

SERVES 4 TO 6

These sautéed bananas are true comfort food — perfect as an accompaniment to Honey Vanilla Ice Cream (see recipe, page 42). They're also a yummy dessert on their own with only a little whipped cream on the side. You can substitute ground ginger for the crystallized ginger if you like.

¼ cup	unsalted butter	50 mL
¾ cup	packed brown sugar	175 mL
1 tsp	ground cinnamon	5 mL
1 tsp	crystallized ginger, finely chopped	5 mL
¼ tsp	ground nutmeg	1 mL
4	firm but ripe bananas, peeled and sliced	4

1. In a large saucepan over medium heat, melt butter. Stir in brown sugar and cook, stirring often, for 3 minutes or until bubbling.

2. Stir in cinnamon, ginger and nutmeg. Add bananas and cook, stirring, for 2 minutes or until heated through and tender. Spoon sauce over ice cream. Sauce will keep, covered and refrigerated, for up to 3 days.

Blueberry Sauce

**MAKES 2 CUPS
(500 ML)**

*Nothing is better than a
hot fruit sauce poured
over cold ice cream.
The heat from the sauce
melts the ice cream to
make a sweet and sinful
puddle on your plate.*

Tip: Since blueberries
are naturally sweet, feel
free to omit or reduce
the amount of maple
syrup in this recipe.

3 cups	fresh blueberries	750 mL
1/4 cup	pure maple syrup	50 mL
1/2 tsp	ground cinnamon	2 mL

1. In a medium saucepan, combine blueberries with maple syrup. Bring to simmer. Cook over medium-low heat, stirring constantly, for 4 minutes. Remove from heat. Stir in cinnamon.

2. Serve hot or at room temperature over your favorite ice cream. Try peach ice cream or a decadent chocolate ice cream. Sauce will keep, covered and refrigerated, for up to 1 week.

Blueberry Basics
Blueberries are considered a superfood because they are an excellent source of antioxidants. They also provide dietary fiber, vitamin C and iron.

Pineapple Topping

MAKES 1 CUP (250 mL)

You'll start to salivate when you stir up this sauce on the stove. The buttery brown sugar is the perfect companion to the soft, slushy pineapple.

2 tbsp	unsalted butter	25 mL
3 tbsp	packed brown sugar	45 mL
1	can (10 oz/284 mL) crushed pineapple	1
2 tbsp	dark rum or tequila	25 mL

1. In a medium saucepan over low heat, melt butter. Stir in brown sugar and pineapple. Bring to a simmer. Cook, stirring, until heated through.

2. Stir in rum. Cook, stirring occasionally, for 2 minutes more.

3. Serve warm over your favorite ice cream. It's especially delicious with vanilla. Sauce will keep, covered and refrigerated, for up to 1 week.

Blackberry Coulis

**MAKES 1 CUP
(250 mL)**

Our favorite thing about making coulis is that you can use almost any fruit to make a sophisticated sauce. Here, we've used blackberries and cassis to add that je ne sais quoi to our ice creams.

Serving suggestion:
Blackberries are an easy yet impressive dessert when served with a scoop of vanilla ice cream and drizzled with blackberry coulis.

2 cups	fresh blackberries	500 mL
¼ cup	black currant (cassis) syrup	50 mL
2 tbsp	granulated sugar	25 mL

1. In a food processor or blender, purée blackberries, syrup and sugar until smooth.

2. Using the back of a wooden spoon, press through a fine sieve into a bowl to remove seeds.

3. Serve over your favorite ice cream. Sauce will keep, covered and refrigerated, for up to 1 week.

Blackberry Basics
Blackberries need to be fully ripe to be sweet and juicy. Their many seeds make them a good source of fiber, so omit Step 2 if you want to get more fiber into your diet.

Mango Ginger Coulis

MAKES 1 CUP
(250 mL)

Sometimes the best sauces are the simplest ones. Here, mangos and ginger combine to make an elegant addition to fruity scoops of ice cream.

2 cups	chopped peeled mango	500 mL
½ cup	crystallized ginger	125 mL
	Juice of 1 lime	

1. In a food processor or blender, purée mango, ginger and lime juice until smooth.

2. Chocolate Mousse Ice Cream (see recipe, page 25) goes well with this sauce, but you can serve it over your favorite ice cream or ice. Sauce will keep, covered and refrigerated, for up to 1 week.

Coulis Basics

A coulis is a thick sauce or purée. The fruity ones are great to dab on dessert plates or to drizzle over tarts and pies. Keep them in plastic bottles with a small nozzle for easy squeezing.

Riesling Peach Coulis

This sophisticated coulis is a great way to turn ordinary ice cream into something extraordinary. Try pooling this sauce underneath a scoop of ice cream and topping with a sprig of mint.

2 cups	sliced peeled peaches	500 mL
½ cup	Riesling wine	125 mL
2 tbsp	granulated sugar	25 mL

1. In a food processor or blender, purée peaches, wine and sugar until smooth.

2. Serve over your favorite ice cream. Sauce will keep, covered and refrigerated, for up to 1 week.

Peach Basics
Peaches are one of the world's top four fruits, the others being apples, bananas and oranges.

Easy Last-Minute Peach Cake

- Preheat oven to 350°F (180°C)
- 8-inch (2 L) square baking pan, lightly greased and dusted with flour

1½ cups	all-purpose flour	375 mL
1 tbsp	baking powder	15 mL
¼ tsp	salt	1 mL
2	eggs	2
1 cup	granulated sugar	250 mL
½ cup	vegetable oil	125 mL
½ tsp	vanilla	2 mL
½ cup	orange juice	125 mL

Topping

½ cup	packed brown sugar	125 mL
1 tbsp	all-purpose flour	15 mL
2 tsp	ground cinnamon	10 mL
¼ cup	melted butter	50 mL
2	ripe peaches, peeled and thinly sliced	2
	Riesling Peach Coulis (see recipe, opposite)	

1. In a small bowl, combine flour, baking powder and salt.

2. In a large bowl, beat eggs, sugar, oil, and vanilla until well combined. Fold in flour mixture until evenly moistened. Stir in orange juice.

3. Prepare the topping: In a small bowl, combine brown sugar, flour and cinnamon. Stir in butter until topping is crumbly.

4. Pour batter into prepared pan and arrange peaches on top. Sprinkle with topping. Bake in preheated oven for 30 minutes or until topping is golden and a tester inserted in the center of the cake comes out clean. Let cool in pan on a wire rack for 10 minutes.

5. Serve warm, with ice cream of your choice and a drizzle of Riesling Peach Coulis.

❧ **SERVES 6**

Strawberry Lime Coulis

Although this sweet-and-sour coulis is the perfect topper to any single-flavor ice cream, the zing of the lime is particularly refreshing when it hits a scoop of classic vanilla.

2 cups	sliced fresh strawberries	500 mL
1/4 cup	granulated sugar	50 mL
	Zest and juice of 1 lime	

1. In a food processor or blender, purée strawberries, sugar and lime juice until smooth.

2. Using the back of a wooden spoon, press through a fine sieve into a bowl to remove seeds. Stir in lime zest. Sauce will keep, covered and refrigerated, for up to 1 week.

✿ Variation

Strawberry Lime Dressing: Use half the amount of sugar, or omit it entirely. Double the amount of lime juice. Mix ingredients well. Serve drizzled over summer fruit or spinach leaves.

Library and Archives Canada Cataloguing in Publication

Linton, Marilyn
    The ice cream bible / Marilyn Linton & Tanya Linton

Includes index
ISBN 978-0-7788-0179-5

    1. Ice cream, ices, etc. I. Linton, Tanya II. Title.

TX795.L55 2008   641.8'62   C2007-907108-2

Index